Brazil and the Challenge of Economic Reform

Brazil and the Challenge of Economic Reform

Edited by Werner Baer and Joseph S. Tulchin

Published by The Woodrow Wilson Center Press

Distributed by The Johns Hopkins University Press

Woodrow Wilson Center Special Studies

The Woodrow Wilson Center Press
Editorial Offices
370 L'Enfant Promenade, S.W.
Suite 704
Washington, D.C. 20024-2518 U.S.A.
telephone 202-287-3000, ext. 218

Distributed by
The Johns Hopkins University Press
Hampden Station
Baltimore, Maryland 21211
order department telephone 1-800-537-5487

Printed in the United States of America

♾ Printed on acid-free paper.

9 8 7 6 5 4 3 2 1

Library of Congress Cataloging-in-Publication Data

Brazil and the challenge of economic reform / edited by Werner Baer and Joseph S. Tulchin.
p. cm. — (Woodrow Wilson Center special studies)
Includes bibliographical references and index.
ISBN 0-943875-53-6 (pbk : alk. paper) : $13.95
1. Brazil—Economic conditions—1964–1985—Congresses. 2. Brazil—Economic conditions—1985– —Congresses. 3. Brazil—Economic policy—Congresses. 4. Economic forecasting—Brazil—Congresses. 5. Brazil—Politics and government—1964–1985—Congresses. 6. Brazil—Politics and government—1985—Congresses. I. Baer, Werner, 1931– . II. Tulchin, Joseph S., 1939– . III. Series.
HC187.B86575 1993
338.981—dc20 93-30786
CIP

The Woodrow Wilson International Center for Scholars

Board of Trustees

The Center is the "living memorial" of the United States of America to the nation's twenty-eighth president, Woodrow Wilson. The U.S. Congress established the Woodrow Wilson Center in 1968 as an international institute for advanced study, "symbolizing and strengthening the fruitful relationship between the world of learning and the world of public affairs." The Center opened in 1970 under its own presidentially appointed board of directors.

Woodrow Wilson Center Special Studies

The work of the Center's Fellows, Guest Scholars, and staff and presentations and discussions at the Center's conferences, seminars, and colloquia often deserve timely circulation as contributions to public understanding of issues of national and international importance. The Woodrow Wilson Center Special Studies series is intended to make such materials available by the Woodrow Wilson Center Press to interested scholars, practitioners, and other readers. In all its activities, the Woodrow Wilson Center is a nonprofit, nonpartisan organization, supported financially by annual appropriations from the U.S. Congress, and by the contributions of foundations, corporations, and individuals. Conclusions or opinions expressed in Center publications and programs are those of the authors and speakers and do not necessarily reflect the views of the Center's staff, Fellows, Trustees, advisory groups, or any individuals or organizations that provide financial support to the Center.

Contents

Figures

Tables

Preface

This volume is the fruit of collaboration between the Latin American Program of the Woodrow Wilson International Center for Scholars and the World Economy Center of the Fundação Getulio Vargas in Rio de Janeiro, Brazil. The project began with a suggestion from Gilberto Dupas that the economic reform program launched by the administration of President Fernando Collor de Mello provided an excellent opportunity to discuss in a public forum the challenges facing the Brazilian economy. The idea was to have a group of distinguished Brazilian analysts meet in Washington, D.C., to offer their thoughts on Brazil's reform process in order to stimulate discussion among representatives of international financial institutions, the Brazilianists among the think tanks and universities in the Washington, D.C., area, and members of the U.S. government interested in Brazil and in the economic restructuring of Latin America.

Several months before the conference, Margaret Daly Hayes, a consultant to the Latin American Program, and I traveled to Rio to meet with the authors of the papers. We sought through this meeting to ensure that chapters would be written in a common format and address the same questions so that public discussion would be more focused and the book we intended to produce would be more coherent. The conference was held on October 18, 1991, and included Werner Baer, Eliana Cardoso, Riordan Roett, and Thomas Skidmore as commentators. The commentators were responsible for stimulating a lively discussion that included the audience and pointed the way to further revision of the papers.

Werner Baer agreed to edit the papers and to write the introduction, putting the chapters of the book into a common context and providing some historical background for the reform effort. Then, at the last moment, because of the dramatic events surrounding the impeachment of President Collor, José Augusto Guilhon Albuquerque wrote the epilogue to ensure that the volume did not appear anachronistic.

I am grateful to all those mentioned for their help in putting this volume together. Special thanks go to Gilberto Dupas, who coordinated the entire project and has supported our efforts to publish the book. In addition, I want to thank Silvia Raw, our former program associate, for helping to organize the event. Gary Bland, our current program associate, put his editing and writing skills to work in preparing the manuscript, and Lucy Hetrick, our program assistant, was, as always, indispensable in organizing the conference.

Joseph S. Tulchin

Abbreviations

ALADI	Latin American Integration Association
BNDE	National Economic Development Bank
CACEX	Foreign Trade Office, Bank of Brazil
CAUCE	Argentina-Uruguay Agreement on Economic Cooperation
CEPAL	United Nations Economic Commission for Latin America and the Caribbean
CIF	charge-in-freight
CNPq	National Research Council
CNI	National Industry Federation
CNP	National Petroleum Council
CONTEL	National Council on Telecommunications
DNAEE	National Department of Water and Electricity
DNC	National Department of Fuels
EEC	European Economic Community
EFTA	European Free Trade Association
EMS	European Monetary System
FDI	foreign direct investment
FEISP	São Paulo State Federation of Industries
FINEP	Funding Authority for Studies and Projects
FNDCT	National Fund for Science and Technology
FTA	free trade area
FUP	Prices Uniformization Fund
GATT	General Agreement on Tariffs and Trade
GDP	gross domestic product
GFFC	gross formation of fixed capital
GNP	gross national product
IGP–DI	general price index
ISI	import-substitution industrialization

JCRR	Joint Commission on Rural Reconstruction
LPG	liquid petroleum gas
MERCOSUR	Common market of Brazil, Argentina, Uruguay, and Paraguay
NAFTA	North American Free Trade Agreement
NATO	North Atlantic Treaty Organization
NICs	newly industrializing countries
OECD	Organization for Economic Cooperation and Development
OID1	Outward-oriented industrial development, 1
OID2	Outward-oriented industrial development, 2
PADCT	Program for the Support of Scientific and Technological Development
PEC	trade expansion program between Uruguay and Brazil
PRN	Fernando Collor's party
RENCOR	General Revision Account for Cleaning of Returns

Contributors

José Augusto Guilhon Albuquerque
Professor of Political Science
University of São Paulo

José Tavares de Araujo, Jr.
Operations Department
Inter-American Development Bank

Fernando de Holanda Barbosa
Professor of Economics and Research Director
Fundação Getulio Vargas

Werner Baer
Professor of Economics
University of Illinois

Gilberto Dupas
Institute of Advanced Studies
University of São Paulo

Luciano Martins
Professor of Political Science
State University of Campinas

Amaury Porto de Oliveira
Visiting Professor
Institute of Advanced Studies
University of São Paulo

Wilson Suzigan
Professor of Economics
Institute of Economics
State University of Campinas

Joseph S. Tulchin
Director
Latin American Program
Woodrow Wilson International Center for Scholars

Introduction

Werner Baer

This book contains the papers presented at the conference "Brazil: The Challenge of Economic Reform," which was held on October 18, 1991, at the Woodrow Wilson International Center for Scholars, sponsored by the Fundacão Getulio Vargas. One major theme running through this conference—the papers presented and the discussions based on them—concerned the types of adjustments necessary to create a new development model and the political feasibility of achieving it by the turn of the century. A related question addressed the reasons for which Brazil has remained mired in a state of political and economic stagnation that has made it unable to emulate the reforms and return to growth of other Latin American countries. The second, closely related theme concerned the economic stagnation and frequent crises of the 1980s and the sociopolitical impasse of the early 1990s, which were seen to reflect in large part the end of the import-substitution-industrialization (ISI) development model that had prevailed since the 1930s.

The effort to achieve industrialization through import substitution began in the 1930s and was fully developed in the two decades following World War II.[1] This effort involved an elaborate system of protection, reliance on foreign direct investment in advanced industrial sectors, the creation and growth of state firms in heavy industries and public utilities, the creation of a development bank (BNDE)[2] to finance both state and private investment projects; and a system of economic and social regulations whose complexity grew over time. The ISI model led to long periods of rapid economic growth and resulted in the structural transformation of the Brazilian economy from the 1930s to the end of the 1970s. In the 1930s industry became the leading growth sector. Its contribution to GDP had surpassed that of agriculture by the 1950s, and by the 1980s industry's share was over three times as large as that of agriculture.

By the 1960s, however, it had already become evident that ISI had failed to solve many of Brazil's socioeconomic problems and that it had engendered many new ones. The capital-intensive nature of ISI resulted in a relatively low rate of industrial job creation in the urban centers, whose population was growing at explosive rates. The capital intensity of industry, the economy's most dynamic sector, also helps to explain how ISI contributed to the worsening of Brazil's distribution of income over the last half century. By the mid-1960s policymakers were forced to adopt programs of export diversification in response to the indiscriminate stress on import substitution, the neglect of exports, and the realization that the level of imports relative to the size of the economy could not be further compressed but was actually rising as a result of the growing industrial sector's need for imported inputs. The stress on ISI resulted in the neglect or worsening of existing problems as well: the regional concentration of economic growth, the stagnation of agriculture, the precarious deficiencies in health care and education, and the ineffectiveness of public administration. The last of these, in part, explains the inflation that accompanied the ISI process.

The military regime that governed Brazil from 1964 to 1985 dealt only partially with some of these post-ISI problems. Through special tax incentives and subsidized credits a dramatic diversification of exports was achieved; tax incentives were also used to stimulate investments in backward regions, to develop capital markets, and to stimulate various types of economic activities. The widespread use of indexation stimulated savings by encouraging people to buy indexed government bonds and to place savings in indexed savings accounts. Indexation was also used to justify the creation of various workers' retirement funds, which amounted to forced savings. Indexed bonds made it temporarily possible for the government to finance deficits in a noninflationary manner and for the development bank to use the forced indexed savings deposits to make long-term loans to strategic public- and private-sector companies. The net result in the late 1960s and 1970s was a period of significant investment in industry and infrastructure projects.

It is noteworthy that the military governments were in a position to keep wage demands in check and even reduce real wages during the austerity years following the takeover in 1964. It is also important to note that the large and growing presence of the state in those years was relatively efficient because state firms were given free play to charge tariffs that enabled them to finance a large part of their investment activities and were not forced to employ more workers than needed. Substantial investments were also made in modernizing and diversifying agriculture, especially in the center-south and in the newly cultivated lands of the western frontier regions, and considerable efforts were made to stimulate technological research (through such institutions as the National Research Council—CNPq—and the Funding Authority for Studies and Projects—FINEP) in a number of elite universities.

Throughout the adjustments under the military, however, relatively little was done to improve the country's concentrated distribution of income and assets and to open the economy to international competition.

Brazil's reaction to the oil shock in late 1973 was to continue pursuing growth through debt. The government promoted ISI programs in the capital goods industry, made substantial investments in energy, and encouraged further export diversification. The oil shock also resulted in a resurgence of inflation, which had reached a low point in 1973. This resurgence can be interpreted, in part, as a consequence of the gradual political opening that the military allowed from 1974 on. In an effort to avoid confrontations among the various socioeconomic groups in the fight for shares of income the government became increasingly willing to allow increased costs (at first resulting from higher energy prices) to be passed on from firm to firm, from wage earners to firms, and so on.[3]

The second oil shock of 1979 and the interest rate shock of 1980–1981 led to the "lost decade" of the 1980s, which was characterized by low rates of economic growth, low rates of investment, high rates of inflation (bordering on hyperinflation), various failed stabilization programs (including some of the heterodox variety), and a decline in foreign resource inflow, which, combined with debt service obligations, resulted for many years in a net transfer of resources out of Brazil. Ironically, Brazil returned to democratic rule in the 1980s. It is impressive that a decade of stagnation and falling living standards did not result in a backsliding to authoritarianism. Less impressive is the inability of the democratic regimes to come to grips with some of the country's basic problems: the highly concentrated distribution of income and the increasingly inefficient state sector, whose performance worsened since the last years of the 1970s as state enterprises were used as instruments of macroeconomic policies, as the state sector was used to provide political favors, and as no consensus could be reached about the distribution of tax burdens among various groups.

The linkage between the debt burden and the growing inflation in the 1980s dramatically illustrated Brazil's lack of social cohesion. Since the foreign debt was mostly that of the government, it was increasingly incumbent on the state to spend domestic currency on the purchase of foreign exchange. The fast-rising expenditure in this category could be financed through either a drastic curtailment of other expenditures or a rise in taxes. Neither of these alternatives was politically acceptable. Because there was a limit to the sale of indexed government financial instruments, inflationary borrowing from the central bank and very short-term borrowing from financial markets (that is, overnight finance, which was equivalent to money) were the only way out. Willingness to accept inflation rather than reduce expenditures or increase taxes clearly showed a lack of social consensus on how the real burden of the debt was to be shared among various social classes.

Even the dramatic experiment of President Collor in 1991, which froze 80 percent of financial assets in order to force an overnight end to inflation, failed in large part because of a lack of social and political consensus. But with a changing world—the collapse of communism and the willingness of an increasing number of developing countries to accept market economics—the Collor program to open the Brazilian economy to trade and investment and to privatize a large segment of state enterprises was grudgingly accepted by most sociopolitical groups.

Brazil in the early 1990s thus found itself at a crossroads. It was groping for a new development model that would provide both the opportunity for renewed economic growth and the prospect of a greater degree of equity.

The chapters of this book concentrate on various aspects of the challenges Brazil faces as it tries to adjust its political and economic system to the post–cold war world. In Chapter 1 Gilberto Dupas proposes a new growth paradigm for the Brazilian economy. He justifies such an approach as a way to overcome the causes of the present economic crisis, which he relates to the collapse of the growth model based on the "trichotomy" of ISI, public investment, and foreign capital, and the recent major international changes in both technological and geopolitical contexts. Given this diagnosis, the new paradigm should be founded on three other components: opening up the economy, reducing the presence of the public sector in the economy, and developing a new industrial policy that favors the transfer of state-of-the-art technology to the country.

Chapter 2, by Luciano Martins, demonstrates how the socioeconomic model of the ISI era has become archaic and how changes in the international arena in the 1980s have made the traditional nationalism-populism movements and the large role of the state in the economy obsolete. In Chapter 3 Amaury Porto de Oliveira contrasts Brazil and other Latin American countries with such Asian countries as South Korea and Taiwan. Among the major differences, he stresses the special aid the Asian countries received from the United States in the 1950s and their much smaller reliance on direct foreign investments. He stresses the opportunities for participating in regional blocs, like MERCOSUR, to attract and develop more modern technology.

It is clear from these chapters that the decline in protection and the withdrawal of special export incentive measures will require a dramatic change in the behavior of the private sector. To survive in the international competitive milieu, firms will have to pay greater attention to increasing their efficiency, obtaining advanced technology, and relying less on various types of government subsidies. The elimination of the distortions resulting from state intervention, which are well described in Chapter 4, by Fernando de Holanda Barbosa, will negatively affect various socioeconomic groups who will be forced to compensate their costs to the economy by increasing the efficiency of their activities.

The future economic role of Brazil in a more open world economy is not too hard to imagine—its large and varied resources will allow it to export a great variety of food products and raw materials; a modernized industrial base will make it possible to export finished and semifinished manufactured products. The major challenge lies in the reorganization of its private and public institutions. In a more privatized and open economy the role of the state will be to concentrate on the education and health of the population and to develop a system of public finance that can lead to greater equity without inhibiting growth. The private sector will have to learn to function without the special protection of the state and without special access to subsidized credits. As is clear from José Tavares de Araujo, Jr.'s, discussion of the MERCOSUR in Chapter 5, greater regional cooperation will necessitate the decline of some sectors, as required by interregional specialization, and the transfer of some policy-making sovereignty to an international organization. And finally, as Chapter 6, by Wilson Suzigan, demonstrates, a system of incentives will have to be developed to make it worthwhile for firms to spend considerable resources on research and development. In general, Brazil's society will have to accept a system in which merit rather than special connections prevails.

The still-unanswered question is whether Brazil has the political will and consensus to adapt its institutions to a new world reality. For instance, how will the Brazilian state address the need to raise the standard of living of its huge poor population? Besides policies leading to more rapid growth, a way will have to be found to finance more intensive investment programs in health, education, and infrastructure. Can a consensus be found to finance such needs through a tax system fairer both in rates and in the mode of collection? Can this be achieved, in part, by making the central bank independent and thus making it impossible for the state to finance its needs in an inflationary manner? The contributors to this collection have highlighted the dilemmas faced by Brazil. It remains to be seen whether Brazilian society can meet these end-of-the-century challenges.

Notes

[1] For a description and analysis of ISI, see Werner Baer, *The Brazilian Economy: Growth and Development*, 3d ed. (New York: Praeger, 1989); Marcelo de Paiva Abreu, ed. *A Ordem do Progresso: Cem Anos de Política Económica Republicana, 1889–1989* (Rio de Janeiro: Editora Campus, 1990).

[2] Banco Nacional de Desenvolvimento Económico. In the 1980s it was renamed Banco Nacional de Desenvolvimento Económico e Social (BNDES).

[3] For a description of the fight-for-shares interpretation of Brazil's resurgence of inflation, see Baer, op. cit., chap. 7; Luiz Carlos Bresser Pereira and Yoshiaki Makano, *Inflação e Recessão* (São Paulo: Editora Brasiliense, 1984); and Werner Baer, "Social Aspects of Latin American Inflation," in Werner Baer, Joseph Petry, and Murray Simpson, eds., *Latin America: The Crisis of the Eighties and the Opportunities of the Nineties* (Champaign: University of Illinois, Bureau of Economic and Business Research, 1991), 45–57.

Chapter 1

Competitive Integration and Recovery of Growth: Risks and Prospects[1]

Gilberto Dupas

The 1980s marked the beginning of the so-called crisis of the Brazilian economy. The most significant signs of this phenomenon can be found in the loss of the economy's vitality and in the rise of chronic inflation. The figures speak for themselves. The accrued growth of the gross domestic product (GDP) throughout the 1980s was only 17 percent, which held the per capita GDP on a plateau of US$2,000 per year. In the 1970s, in contrast, the Brazilian economy grew almost 130 percent—which represents a *yearly* average of 7.2 percent (Table 1.1).

Inflation in its turn became chronic[2] and turned into perhaps the greatest obstacle to a return to sustainable growth for the Brazilian economy (Table 1.2). Inflation rates considerably above those deemed bearable by developed countries are not new to the Brazilian economy. The coerced withdrawal of savings to accelerate industrialization (accomplished through monetary expansion to finance the public deficit), the oligopolistic supply structure, and Brazil's traditional monetary liberalism are some of the elements that have been nourishing Brazilian inflation since the 1930s.

Over the years some mechanisms have been created to make inflation bearable.[3] Monetary correction assured greater protection of financial savings and broadened the possibilities of noninflationary financing for the public sector; minidevaluations of the cruzeiro impeded exaggerated fluctuations of the exchange rate and guaranteed a normal flow of foreign trade; and,

TABLE 1.1
ECONOMIC GROWTH—GDP
(Real Rates of Variation)

Year	GDP—real rate—%	Population (million)	Per capita DP in 1989 US$
1971	11.3	98.2	1,230.67
1973	14.0	103.0	1,496.42
1975	5.2	108.0	1,624.78
1976	10.3	110.6	1,750.55
1979	6.8	118.6	1,921.07
1980	9.2	121.3	2,050.54
1981	(4.4)	124.1	1,916.36
1982	0.7	126.9	1,886.74
1983	(3.4)	129.8	1,782.31
1984	5.0	132.7	1,830.61
1985	0.3	135.6	1,940.07
1986	7.5	138.5	2,041.47
1987	3.6	141.5	2,070.72
1988	0.0	144.4	2,028.05
1989	3.6	147.4	2,058.64
1990	(4.3)	150.4	1,924.82
1991	1.2	153.4(*p*)[a]	1,923.28(*p*)[a]

SOURCE: Economic Program—Government of Brazil, 1991.
[a](*p*)—preliminary.

TABLE 1.2
INFLATION—SELECTED INDICATORS
(Annual Variation)

Year	General price index—domestic supply	Extended national consumer price index	National consumer price index
1977	38.8	NA	NA
1978	40.8	NA	NA
1979	77.2	NA	NA
1980	110.2	99.2	99.7
1981	95.2	95.6	93.5
1982	99.7	104.8	100.3
1983	211.0	164.0	178.0
1984	223.8	215.3	209.1
1985	235.1	242.2	239.0
1986	65.0	75.5	58.6
1987	415.8	374.0	396.0
1988	1,037.6	981.1	994.3
1989	1,782.9	1,972.9	1,863.6
1990	1,476.6	1,621.0	1,585.2
1991	480.2	472.7	475.1

SOURCE: Economic Program—Government of Brazil, 1991.

finally, the automatic adjustment of salaries, albeit not sufficient to avoid decreases in their actual value, gave leeway to long-term agreements and secured the continuity of production.

The novelty of the 1980s was thus not inflation itself but the change in its profile and the fact that there was now a concrete risk that control of the monetary system would be lost.

Despite the expectations aroused by his election, the investiture of President Collor in 1990 did not bring material changes to this picture. New attempts to control inflation by means of shocks also failed, and the performance of the economy in 1990–1992 was only a little better than poor.[4] Over this period the GNP dropped 3.1 percent, with a particularly unfavorable impact on the industrial sector.

The interruption of growth and the chronic inflation are the more evident symptoms of extreme unbalance in the structure of the Brazilian economy. They reflect the exhaustion of the development model that led to the formation of the country's industrial complex and to the radical transformation of its structures (economic, political, and social) over the past sixty years.

Briefly stated, this model was grounded on three basic factors:

1. The mobilizing role of the public sector, which assumed the duties of coordinating, funding, and creating the infrastructure required for the installation of the industrial complex;
2. The existence of a national development project, although it was not always clear that its basic purpose was the formation of a complete and integrated industrial capacity similar to that of more developed countries; as a by-product of this project, the strategy of replacing imports took on the role of an industrial policy; and
3. The existence of an external environment that was, more often than not, favorable either for attracting risk capital (mainly in the 1950s and 1960s) or for obtaining financial loans (already in the 1970s) to offset the trade deficit and balance foreign accounts.

The Brazilian crisis is rooted in the effects of these three basic factors. The development model built from them is no longer capable of offering dynamism to the Brazilian economy. Finding a solution to Brazil's economic problems is not, therefore, simply a matter of reviewing this model or of trying to repair its faults but of finding a new model with other foundations.

This study is part of this search for a new development model that will enable the Brazilian economy to return to a pattern of growth and competitive integration into the new international economic environment.

This study has three parts: the first briefly surveys the conditions leading to the impairment of each of the factors that determined the previous model. Our purpose here is not to be original but to determine the central elements of this process and find elements to formulate a new model. The second part analyzes recent changes in the international environment in order to identify their possible impact on the Brazilian economy. The third and final part of the study is an attempt to identify which basic contours could be used for a new development model. The study focuses on the need to find a new industrial strategy; in it we analyze the risks and prospects of such a strategy as well as the manner in which it might be integrated into the world economy.[5]

The Downfall of the Growth Model[6]

THE BANKRUPTCY OF THE PUBLIC SECTOR

In Brazil, as in other countries of late or delayed industrialization, the government has always played a fundamental role in promoting economic development. The industrialization challenges of the 1920s were too complex to be faced by private enterprise alone. The already significant technological evolution of more developed countries, the need to broaden the country's basic infrastructure, and the high cost of new investments made the participation of the public sector indispensable to industrialization. The Brazilian government was reasonably efficient on all these fronts. From the nationalism of Getúlio Vargas (1930–1945 and 1951–1954), to the development-minded performance of Juscelino Kubitschek (1956–1960), to the military government's dream of a strong Brazil (1964–1985), the public sector clearly furthered industrialization and development.[6]

In its role of coordinator and articulator, the government indicated the goals to be achieved and the space to be occupied by foreign capital. The installation of the automotive industry during Kubitschek's government is a classic example of this division of duties among foreign capital, national private capital, and public-sector capital under the government's command.

As a lender, the government did not hesitate to advance credits and grant subsidies for the formation of private-sector capital; and, through its state companies, it took charge of setting up the infrastructure required for the industrialization project. The public sector concentrated on energy, transportation, and basic resources, where the risks and the capital necessary for investment are high and the maturation period is long.[7]

In spite of the problems created by the government's performance (low efficiency of the majority of investments, excessive regulations, corruption, and so forth), the result was positive, at least until the mid-1970s. It was exactly at this time, starting with the oil crisis and increasing international interest rates, that the problems of the public sector began. Table 1.3 provides some figures that illustrate the downgrading of Brazilian public finances as the 1970s came to an end. The savings of the public sector, which in the 1970s remained around 6 to 7 percent of GDP, dropped progressively until they reached a deficit of 5.3 percent of GDP in 1989, the last year of Sarney's government. The gravity of the Brazilian fiscal crisis can be seen in the figures for the 1990s; all the effort of the Collor government, including the new taxes, postponement of expenses, and freezing of financial assets produced only a temporary and partial balance of public finances.

Briefly, this means that the bankruptcy of the Brazilian public sector can be attributed to three basic factors:

1. The foreign debt crisis and the increased cost of rolling over foreign and domestic debts. Payments on account of foreign debt interest, which amounted to less than 0.5 percent of GDP in the 1970s, reached 3.5 percent of GDP in 1989;[8]
2. Spiraling inflation, which significantly reduced the actual tax burden. It is known that inflation mainly "attacks" indirect taxes (as a result of the so-called Tanzi effect), exactly where the tax burden is concentrated in Brazil; and
3. A significant increase, at the close of the 1980s, in expenses of salaries and wages, primarily in states and municipalities. To make this picture even grimmer, the new constitution changed tax distribution among the three governmental spheres without materially modifying the

Table 1.3 Current Account Government Savings (Percentage of GDP)

	Gross Tax Load			Transfers						Government Consumption					
										Personnel					
Year	Indirect taxes (1)	Direct taxes (2)	Total (3)	Domestic public debt interest[a] (4)	Foreign debt interest (5)	Socal welfare (6)	Subsidy (7)	Total (8)	Net revenue[b] (9 = 3 − 8)	Central government (10)	States and municipalities (11)	Total (12)	Goods and services (13)	Total (14)	Government savings (15 = 9 − 14)
1970	17.01	9.28	26.29	0.52	0.05	8.25	0.52	9.34	16.95	4.18	4.07	8.25	3.09	11.34	5.61
1971	15.50	9.69	25.19	0.39	0.08	6.98	0.78	8.23	16.96	4.07	4.46	8.53	2.71	11.24	5.72
1972	15.56	10.37	25.93	0.29	0.17	7.20	0.58	8.24	17.69	3.46	4.32	7.78	2.88	10.66	7.03
1973	14.65	10.35	25.00	0.39	0.10	6.64	1.17	8.30	16.70	3.54	3.50	7.04	2.93	9.97	6.73
1974	14.77	10.34	25.11	0.40	0.09	6.04	2.15	8.68	16.43	2.95	3.49	6.44	2.95	9.39	7.04
1975	13.90	11.33	25.23	0.38	0.19	6.76	2.67	10.00	15.23	3.33	3.81	7.14	3.05	10.19	5.04
1976	13.46	11.63	25.09	0.49	0.18	7.22	1.53	9.42	15.67	3.43	3.73	7.16	3.30	10.46	5.21
1977	13.36	12.19	25.55	0.48	0.16	7.26	1.48	9.38	16.17	3.13	3.45	6.58	2.85	9.43	6.74
1978	13.38	12.30	25.68	0.47	0.19	8.13	1.88	10.67	15.01	3.12	3.79	6.91	2.76	9.67	5.34
1979	12.21	12.45	24.66	0.55	0.29	7.80	1.91	10.55	14.11	2.89	4.09	6.98	2.92	9.90	4.21
1980	13.52	11.18	24.70	0.76	0.37	7.77	3.86	12.76	11.94	2.76	3.55	6.31	2.89	9.20	2.74
1981	12.92	11.73	24.65	1.08	0.29	8.22	2.68	12.27	12.38	2.96	3.50	6.46	2.86	9.32	3.06
1982	12.57	12.69	25.26	1.17	1.14	8.58	2.48	13.37	11.89	3.02	4.03	7.05	2.96	10.01	1.88
1983	12.81	12.26	25.07	1.55	1.56	8.36	2.65	14.12	10.95	2.89	3.72	6.61	3.05	9.66	1.29
1984	10.43	11.39	21.82	2.08	1.76	7.76	1.59	13.19	8.63	2.47	3.18	5.65	2.63	8.28	0.35
1985	10.57	11.96	22.53	2.30	1.51	7.24	1.59	12.64	9.89	3.06	3.88	6.94	2.93	9.87	0.02
1986	12.47	12.88	25.35	1.19	1.35	7.97	1.47	11.98	13.37	2.40	4.90	7.30	3.37	10.67	2.70
1987	11.59	11.76	23.35	1.01	1.42	7.54	1.59	11.56	11.79	2.78	4.99	7.77	4.39	12.16	−0.37
1988	10.89	11.00	21.89	1.58	1.72	7.18	1.23	11.71	10.18	3.21	4.71	7.92	4.68	12.60	−2.42
1989	10.77	11.17	21.94	1.44	2.03	7.50	1.93	12.90	9.04	4.11	5.61	9.72	4.60	14.32	−5.28
1990	14.31	13.12	27.43	−1.09	2.12	8.29	1.72	11.04	16.39	3.63	6.86	10.49	5.15	15.64	0.75

SOURCE: Brazilian Institute of Geography and Statistics (IBGE).

[a] Up to 1982, interest on Brazil's foreign debt corresponds to concepts used by the IBGE Foundation, discounting OTN monetary correction and the LTN discount. From 1983 onward, service on both the domestic and the foreign debt was estimated on the basis of an average balance of the public-sector debt.

[b] Does not include other current net revenues, as these are basically the result of monetary correction.

charges and expenses. As a result, it became practically impossible for the federal government to balance the budget.

The result is already known. The Brazilian state not only lost its investment and growth leadership capability but also had no means of financing its debts without creating inflation.

In addition to this quantitative dimension, the depletion of the public sector has a noteworthy qualitative aspect. For all practical purposes, technological innovation, the speed of data transmission, and the swiftness of business transactions in the present world have negated the possibility of a close collaboration between government and business. This knowledge has given impetus to privatization all over the world, and Brazil certainly cannot insulate itself from this tendency. Reducing the size of the public sector and redirecting it to the tasks of furthering and monitoring business activities in the private sector can hardly be avoided.

The Depletion of the Import Substitution Model[9]

As mentioned earlier, under the development model that shaped Brazil's present economic situation, the strategy of replacing imports took on the role of an industrial policy. The purpose of this strategy, although not always clearly delineated, was to set up an industrial complex supposedly like those of developed countries: integrated, dynamic, and virtually nondependent on imports. The country's advantages included a great quantity of cheap labor, the availability of raw materials, and an attractive domestic market for a developing economy. In fact, the scale of the Brazilian market was comparable only to that of developed countries. And the government's commitment to the heavy taxation of imported products that had Brazilian equivalents made the installation of industrial plants in the country appealing.

The result of this choice was the formation of a reasonably complete and integrated industrial complex, but with a series of problems: very low efficiency and productivity rates, excessive protection against foreign competition, reduced markets thwarting competition and economies of scale, and a low level of investment in product research and development. The Brazilian automotive industry, which has sales of approximately 11 percent of GDP and constitutes the country's most important industrial segment, provides a perfect example of the problems inherent in this option. It is characterized by low efficiency, outdated technology, a reduced production scale, and little access to foreign markets.[9]

Brazil rates significantly lower on some basic items such as vehicle assembly time, average number of defects, and design age, in comparison not only to the so-called first-world countries but also to countries with similar levels of development, such as South Korea and Mexico (Table 1.4).

Insufficient scale and excessive supply concentration structures are some of the problems shown in Tables 1.5 and 1.6. Brazilian production was stagnant throughout the 1980s. Record levels of production continued in the 1980s, when almost 1.2 million automobiles were assembled. The average number of vehicles assembled per plant per year, however, has never exceeded 130,000, much below the recommended level (200,000), which would allow economies of scale and result in significant productivity gains.

The automotive industry's attempt since its inception to offset the contraction of the domestic market by increasing exports illustrates another basic formation trait of Brazil's industrial complex, the limited opening to foreign markets and the reduced competitiveness of manufactured goods. Foreign sales were stimulated by fiscal incentives and official benefits, including favorable exchange rates; this is the so-called spurious competitiveness based on economic trends and not on comparative structural advantages.[10] When incentives

TABLE 1.4
THE AUTOMOTIVE INDUSTRY WORLDWIDE

Brazil	Japan	Mexico	Korea	United States	Europe
Assembly Time (hours per vehicle)					
48.1	16.0	45.7	30.3	25.1	36.0
Defects per 100 Vehicles					
92.5	60.0	69.0	87.5	82.0	105.0
Age of Design (years)					
11.0	2.0	8.0	4.0	4.0	NA

SOURCE: José Roberto Ferro, "Para Sair da Estagnaçáo e Diminuir o Atraso Tecnológico da Industria Automobílistica Brasileira," (Universidade de Campinas, São Paulo, 1990, mimeographed).

TABLE 1.5
SCALE OF PRODUCTION
IN THE AUTOMOTIVE INDUSTRY
(Vehicles per Day per Plant)

Country	Number
Brazil	600
Japan	1,770
Mexico	400
Korea	1,700
United States	NA
Europe	1,730

SOURCE: José Roberto Ferro, "Para Sair da Estagnação e Diminuir o Atraso Technológico da Industria Automobílistica Brasileira."

TABLE 1.6
PRODUCTION AND EXPORTS IN BRAZIL'S AUTOMOTIVE INDUSTRY

Year	Production	Domestic market	Exports
1979	1,117,966	1,012,318	105,648
1980	1,165,174	1,008,089	157,085
1981	780,883	568,197	212,686
1982	859,304	685,953	173,351
1983	896,462	727,788	168,674
1984	864,653	668,138	196,515
1985	966,708	759,068	207,640
1986	1,056,332	873,053	183,279
1987	920,071	574,516	345,555
1988	1,068,756	748,280	320,476
1989	940,000	NA	NA
1990	850,000	NA	NA

SOURCE: José Roberto Ferro, "Para Sair da Estagnação e Diminuir o Atraso Tecnológico da Industria Automobílistica Brasileira."

disappear, exports decline for lack of competitiveness in international markets. The Brazilian automotive industry, which was already a leader of the national development cycle, is presently stagnant and has practically no chance of becoming part of the new worldwide growth in that sector. As this example shows, the import substitution strategy has had its day as a development project for Brazil.

Although it is technologically outdated, Brazil has an industrial GDP of approximately US$140 billion, a significantly diversified and almost complete industrial complex in its more important segments. Industry thus has a huge "critical mass" on which the current national development standard depends. But the model that set this standard has already completed its mission and become obsolete, mostly as a result of the technological advances of the past decade. It no longer makes sense to overprotect industry that supplies the domestic market on a reduced scale and with serious inefficiency in important sectors of the productive chain.

The need to find some means of competitive integration into the world economy demands the replacement of this model. As we will discuss in the final part of this study, the risks inherent in this course of action are not small—yet there seems to be no other option.

A Reversal of the Foreign Scenario

At least until the beginning of the 1980s, Brazilian industrial development counted on providing a very favorable environment for foreign investment. The flow of foreign resources increased in the 1950s because of a combination of two circumstances: many foreign companies adopted a growth strategy that led them to expand their businesses outside their countries of origin; and the appeal of the domestic market and the facilities offered by the Brazilian government made the country an attractive alternative for foreign risk capital.

Beginning in the 1960s and primarily in the 1970s, the nature of Brazil's articulation with the international economy changed. International creditors began providing loans to Brazil to finance growing deficits in its balance of payments (particularly as of the first oil crisis and the launching of the Second National Development Plan).

This close cooperation with foreign capital was fundamental to Brazilian industrial development but did not modify its nature (overprotective, aimed toward the domestic market, and technologically deficient in innovative vitality). The majority of the multinational companies concentrated their innovations almost exclusively on adapting their products to the specific requirements of the Brazilian market. High import tariffs to guard the market from foreign competition guaranteed significant profit margins, and the technological investment had already been amortized in the multinationals' countries of origin.

These considerations show the limitations, but do not diminish the significance, of foreign capital as one of the pillars of Brazilian industrial development. In the 1980s Brazil switched from being an importer to being an exporter of capital. This is a well-known story. After the second oil crisis and the increase in the interest rates prompted by the U.S. Federal Reserve Board as of 1979 Brazil's foreign indebtedness grew enormously, and foreign banks refused to continue financing the deficits of its balance of payments. From that point on, the country was forced to create through its trade balance the funds (in foreign currency) required to pay for the foreign debt service. At the same time, aggravating these problems even further, risk capital disappeared mainly because Brazil's inflationary spiral and the reduction in its growth rhythm strongly reduced the expected return on new investments. The opposite took place in other international markets, with the renewal of investment opportunities in Europe, in the Far East, and even in advanced segments of U.S. industry.[11]

The Brazilian economy thus had to face an unfavorable foreign environment in which Brazil's creditors tried to protect themselves as much as possible from exposure and new capital preferred to invest elsewhere.

The Changes in the International Environment

While the Brazilian economy suffers the consequences of the obsolesence of its development model, the world economy is undergoing intense transformation. Economically, the beginning of this process can be found in the mid-1970s, when the developed countries (mainly Europe and Japan) began to implement their programs for the industrial restructuring of their economies. More recently, political and ideological transformations have occurred as well—most significantly, the dismantling of socialism and the consequent end of the cold war.

Changes are in progress, and it is still too early to define precisely the new contours of the international environment in the years to come. However, it is already possible to identify some basic trends.

THE ROLE OF TECHNOLOGICAL INNOVATION

The first trend involves technological innovation and the renewal of the technical basis of the more developed capitalist countries.[12] The creation and diffusion of new technology, mainly in microelectronics, computerization, biotechnology, and new materials, has had a decisive impact on the guidelines for operating the world economy. Technological innovations have not been limited to the creation of new products in the advanced sectors of the economy. They have also involved more mature segments (previously reliant on labor or cheap energy) in which the developed countries had lost their strength and competitiveness. Consequently, it is important to review the concept of comparative advantages. The advantages enjoyed by poorer countries—the availability of raw materials, natural energy sources, and cheap labor—lost a great deal of their strategic importance as in the great majority of cases they have been offset by the gains in productivity and efficiency achieved through new technology.[13]

Growing financial costs and the risks associated with research and technological innovation should accelerate the preparation of the economy for worldwide competition. In the more dynamic segments a predominantly oligopolistic economic structure is likely to be consolidated, assisted by international operating agreements among large corporations. These types of agreements, which the automotive industry has been using in recent years, reduce risks and accelerate the amortization of new investments.

THE ROLE OF MACROMARKETS

The second important trend in the new international environment is undoubtedly the formation and likely consolidation of macromarkets or regional economic blocs. The most likely ones are a unified Europe; an American market including the United States, Canada, and Mexico (even though the conditions for inclusion of the last-mentioned country have not yet been defined); and an Asian bloc headed by Japan. Except for the European process, which has made great progress, there are doubts that these blocs are likely to be formed in the short term.

In the medium and long term, however, the progress of economic integration seems inevitable. Even if the formation of totally integrated economic blocs on the European pattern takes considerable time, the establishment of privileged conditions and the concentration of intraregional trade should consolidate more rapidly in order to broaden markets and thus ensure economies of scale in industry that will compensate for the costs associated with technological research and modern commercial strategies.

We are not yet sure about the impact of this transformation on the trade of less developed countries. In principle, it seems reasonable to expect an expansion of intrabloc trade to the detriment of business with nonaffiliated countries. If this happens, it may accelerate the isolation of developing countries, whose participation in world trade has been decreasing significantly in recent years. The figures in Table 1.7 show that the share of the developing countries in total world exports dropped from 29 percent in 1980 to 22 percent in 1988.[14] Nonetheless, European protectionism, for instance, tends to concentrate more on products with significant technological content and less on goods exported from developing countries. Even with this kind of integration, poor countries would clearly remain in a subordinate position. As has been the case traditionally, these countries would continue to face strong variations in the demand and prices of their major products. Thus, economic growth would remain uneven, and prosperity uncertain.

Geopolitical Changes

Finally, the new geopolitical configuration that has begun to prevail since the collapse of the Communist bloc and the end of the cold war is the third vector that should set the boundaries for the international scenario until the turn of the century. The

TABLE 1.7
EXPORTS OF DEVELOPED AND DEVELOPING NATIONS

Year	Developed market economy (% of total world exports)	Developing countries and China (% of total world exports)
1980	63	29
1981	62	30
1982	63	28
1983	64	26
1984	64	26
1985	66	25
1986	70	21
1987	70	22
1988	70	22

SOURCE: Paulo Renato de Souza, "Desafios ao Desenvolvimento Brasiliero," *Revista de Economia Política* 10, no. 2 (April–June 1990): 17–32.

demise of socialism has put an end to the chief ideological division in the world and to the automatic alignment of the majority of countries with either the United States or the Soviet Union.

From a purely pragmatic viewpoint, this new environment seems less favorable to developing countries, particularly in Latin America (obviously excluding Mexico because of its geographical location). In the first place, the number of candidates applying for financing from the rich countries has increased significantly. East Germany's recovery, for instance, will require approximately US$500 billion throughout the next five years. Second, the end of the cold war will virtually eliminate any stimuli for the United States to allocate resources out of strategic interest to Latin American countries. The likely exception will lie in funds for combating drug traffic, which is a minute and localized expenditure that is insufficient to revitalize an economy the size of Brazil's.

THE BRAZILIAN CHALLENGE

Taken together, these changes in the international environment point to increasing difficulties for developing countries in general. Brazil's situation is particularly fragile, even compared to its closest neighbors. If we put aside its domestic troubles, which are not insignificant, the size of the Brazilian economy complicates the process of attracting enough foreign funds to achieve economic revitalization. For the sake of comparison, Chile's GDP is approximately US$30 billion, Uruguay's is only US$9 billion, and even Argentina's national product is only slightly over US$85 billion. Even a marginal proportion of the funds available for investment in the international market can contribute to leading these economies back toward long-term growth. For Brazil, however, with a GDP of approximately US$400 billion and a large industrial complex, a further opening of the economy to international investment will not suffice. It is necessary to establish a new model of development and of integration with the world economy.[15]

The Construction of a New Model

As I have tried to demonstrate in this chapter, the model of development that molded Brazil's industrialization has become obsolete. It is therefore necessary to find a new path that can put the country back on its course to economic growth. The definition of such a development project is an extremely complex task and obviously beyond the scope of this study. As a contribution to this debate, I will try to suggest the basic contours that this new model should have.

The premise is that a new development model should inevitably call for a greater opening of the Brazilian economy and better connection with the economy of the world. This new model will have to reflect the new international environment. The speed of technological innovation, the growing cost [illegible]ved in the research and development of new products, [illegible]he swift transmission of information have caused profound [illegible]ges in the process of economic development.

[illegible]n addition, as the importance of cross-border companies [illegible] grown, it has become practically impossible to attempt au[illegible]nomous development or to base a development model on ex[illegible]ssive protection of companies established in the country. As [illegible]mphasized in an earlier study,

> In fact, if we were always used to hegemonic cycles that lasted for centuries, in the recent past they would not have survived the

> transitory decades. In the near future, however, it is possible that the concept of hegemony will no longer even apply. It is likely that there will only be room for transitory arrangements between dominant blocs negotiated basically according to global strategies established by cross-border corporations. In this scenario of dramatic changes in the international economy, the cross-border character of companies takes on a material role. While seeking relevance in the new large macro-markets and to maintain leadership in technological innovation, corporations have been forced to engage in aggressive policies for mergers, acquisitions, and minority participations.[16]

In accord with the fundamental premise that the Brazilian economy must be opened to foreign markets, two basic tasks must be undertaken in the process of formulating a new development project for the country: reviewing the role of the government in the economy and defining an industrial strategy.

THE ROLE OF THE GOVERNMENT

The Brazilian government shows symptoms similar to the Brazilian economy as a whole: it has a chronic deficit due to excessive debts (which are financed precariously) and to ongoing overspending (mainly in the states and municipalities since the new Constitution was adopted). It is inefficient both in performing typical governmental duties (mainly in the social area) and in regulating the economy and preparing medium- and long-term plans.

To complicate this picture further, although the deficit of the public sector could logically be remedied by higher taxes, corporate taxpayers and the middle class already have far too heavy a tax burden. How can the need for higher fiscal revenue for adjustment of the public sector be reconciled with the existing excessive tax burden? The solution to this dilemma would probably involve a new definition of the tax structure and significant enhancement of public-sector efficiency.

Redefining the tax structure should mean increasing direct taxes, on income and personal assets, and reducing the so-called indirect taxes. Besides being less fair from the social point of view, these taxes encumber investments and transactions in general and lead to less efficiency in the economic system.

Making public expenditure more efficient depends on a thorough review of how the government intervenes in the economy.

On the one hand, it is necessary to bring about a progressive reduction of the collaboration between government and business, having the government concentrate on social areas and on the coordination and inspection of private business activities. On the other hand, it is necessary to increase the efficiency of the government in the social sphere: this will require decentralizing social expenditures to a greater extent by delegating greater responsibilities to states and municipalities. It is likely that bringing the governmental functions closer to the population will permit greater grassroots control (in terms of social justice and efficiency) of the allocation of public resources.

In summary, therefore, we should reduce the size of the government, eliminate its ability to undertake direct economic action (by means of state companies, for instance), and make it more decentralized. On the other hand, the public sector should take on the roles of goad and judge in the economic process: that is, it should stimulate the performance of private agents, define the rules of the game, ascertain compliance with those rules, and punish those who break them.

A New Industrial Society

Once the new role of the government has been defined, the next step would be to formulate a realistic industrial policy to suit the current international environment.

Recent experience in the world has shown that this task would be very difficult without the effective involvement of a capable government. The government's role is to stimulate collaboration by the national and international private sectors in building a new industrial policy that is feasible in view of the prevailing interests and market forces. It does not seem possible simply to let the interaction of market forces define the course of Brazilian industrial development, despite the power of neoliberal economic ideas in today's world. As a matter of fact, examples of countries with successful economic development show that economic planning is not antithetical to market theory. Indeed, these two elements can and must be complementary strengths in accelerating a country's industrial development.[17]

To accomplish the huge task of recycling Brazilian industry, it will be necessary to choose some dynamic sectors on which all the national effort will be concentrated to try to generate the modern and competitive segments that will support the next accumulation cycle. This will obviously require minimum economic stability and intelligent agreements with international capital, using the language these international players know and accept: pragmatism and bargaining.

A significant portion of the current productive capacity will not survive the realities of the market. The portion that does survive will depend on the strategic interests of the multinationals, which regard partnerships with local production as an alternative to consolidating the world macromarkets.

Fortunately, significant sectors with some material competitive advantages to offer—because of either high-quality natural resources or cheap labor—will remain. These sectors, however, require a great deal of attention. Pressured by heavy and cumulative tax burdens, penalized by poorly qualified labor, and disadvantaged abroad by intense automation and high technology with diminishing hardware costs, these advantages are quickly fading and may be doomed. The sectors that should support this new industrial policy should therefore be chosen on the basis of two criteria:

- Their strategic importance in positioning the country to compete in the international market; and
- The degree to which the national industry in each industrial sector or segment has access to advanced technology.

The sectors (or segments) to receive highest priority fall into two major groups, each governed by a different strategy:

1. Industries that involve mature technology in which Brazil has comparative advantages and the command of world-class technology, including some segments of the steel industry, the pulp and paper industry, and portions of the agricultural industry. These industries would require a relatively short-term strategy aimed at maintaining leadership and absorbing new technologies from a position of worldwide hegemony. The export revenues derived from these sectors should, moreover, play a decisive role in securing a significant portion of the foreign exchange required to finance the country's imports; and
2. Advanced industries such as microelectronics, computerization, new materials, and biotechnology that would help

Brazil compete more effectively in the international market. These industries would require a long-term approach that takes into account the strategies of cross-border corporations and takes advantage of opportunities to work with international capital (in partnerships, technological agreements, and the like) for each sector.

In implementing the strategies for promoting both groups of industries, one must consider the system of priorities by which loans are to be granted and the manner in which universities and public and private research centers can be integrated into the development program.

The survival of other sectors will depend entirely on their ability to regain reasonable competitiveness over a rather short period and to provide employment for Brazil's labor force.

This path will naturally not be free of obstacles. In general, two of these obstacles are especially noteworthy:

1. Unemployment in the private industrial sector and in the public sector in the first stages of modernizing the economy. This problem is already being experienced to some degree even though it is unfortunately not part of a modernization program. The potential for further increases in unemployment reinforces the importance of broadening the scope and improving the efficiency of the government's activity in the social sector. It is the only offsetting mechanism that can be triggered at this stage of economic transition until it is possible to reabsorb the mass of workers affected by the process of adjusting the economy; and
2. The possibility that problems will arise in the balance of payments at these initial stages of the program to modernize the economy. Such problems could come about as an increase in imports of machinery, equipment, and technology to modernize the Brazilian industrial complex becomes necessary. It will therefore be essential to define a strategy for overcoming Brazil's foreign exchange vulnerability. To do this, certain steps are fundamental, especially the normalization of relations with the international financial community, including the adoption of a stable agreement for repaying the foreign debt; the intensification of the export effort and a clear policy for the formation of reserves; and finally increases in the facilitation of and appeals for

foreign investment in the country (including the removal of obstacles to investment in sectors that were previously considered strategic, such as mining).

A more general threat to the success of this opening strategy is that the assets of the industrial complex may become scrap without being replaced by new and dynamic economic centers. Even in a favorable scenario, the key to sucess lies in knowing how the modern and the old or decadent sectors are related. Should such asset loss occur, unemployment and the balance of payments would worsen, and the government would most likely be unable to maintain political and social stability.

Conclusion

The guidelines we have provided in this chapter are basically an attempt at redefining the strategy of Brazilian development and its integration into the world economy. We have not tried to formulate an alternative model but only to discuss some basic proposals that may be useful in establishing a program for the reform of the Brazilian economy.

The matters we have discussed clearly involve long-term structural changes that will face numerous obstacles. It is because such changes can be expected to take time that we have not addressed the issue of inflation, not because we believe that the control of inflation will be less important to the recovery of the Brazilian economy. On the contrary, in our opinion, the instability created by inflation presents an almost unsurpassable hindrance to the structural reforms and the new model of development we have proposed.

But those who claim that inflationary control will solve all of Brazil's problems are also making a mistake. After controlling inflation, Brazil will again have to find its way to development. One hopes this study will somehow help to light the way.

Notes

1 Rubens Sardenberg, director of the GRANO EPC economic analysis group, collaborated in the preparation of this text.

2 For an explanation of chronic inflation, see for instance, André Lara Resende, "Da Inflação Cronica a Hiperinflação: Observações Sobre o Quadro Atual," *Revista de Economia Política* 9 (January–March 1989).

[3] More precisely, the risk that the economy will experience hyperinflation only appeared in the second half of the decade. The exhaustion of the indexation tools plus the intensification of structural imbalances led the Brazilian economy on the route to hyperinflation. This was avoided only by repeated price freezes, which destroyed the credibility of the economic policy and the indexation mechanisms.

[4] A broad overview of the first Collor plan can be found in Clovis de Faro, ed., *Plano Collor: Avaliações e Perspectivas,* (São Paulo: Lovros Tecnicos e Científícoes Editora, 1990).

[5] On the government's role in the new model, see João Paulo dos Reis Velloso, editor, *Condições para a Retomada do Desenvolvimento,* (São Paulo: Forum Nacional, Editora Nobel, 1991).

[6] For a competent summary of the development of the Brazilian economy from postwar to the end of the 1970s, see José Serra "Ciclos e Mudanças Estruturais na Economia Brasileira do Pós-Guerra," in Luiz Gonzaga M. Belluzo and Renata Coutinho, editors, *Desenvolvimento Capitalista no Brasil—Ensaios sobre a Crise,* (São Paulo: Editora Brasiliense, 1982). Analysis of the Brazilian economy through the period of transition to democracy can be found in Gilberto Dupas, *Crise Economica e Transiçâsõ Democrática—83/86 A Delicada Trajetoria Brasukeura* (São Paulo: Editora Klaxon, 1987). For an interesting summary of the evolution of the Brazilian economy in the 1980s, see Eliana A. Cardoso and Albert Fishlow, *Macroeconomia de Divida Externa,* (São Paulo: Editora Brasiliense, 1989).

[7] The most important periods for the postwar construction of the Brazilian industrial complex undoubtedly occurred during the government of Juscelino Kubitschek (Goals for 57/60) and of Ernesto Geisel (the "II PND 74/79"). For in-depth analysis of these periods, including the decisive participation of the Brazilian government, see Carlos Lessa, *15 Anos de Política Economica* (São Paulo: Editora Brasiliense, 1981); Antonia Castro and Francisco Eduardo Pires de Barros de Souza, *A Economia Brasileira em Marcha Forada* (Rio de Janeiro: Editora Paz e Terra, 1985).

[8] See Luiz Carlos Bresser Pereira, "Da Crise Fiscal a Redução da Dívida," in L. C. Bresser Pereira, editor, *Dívida Externa: Crise e Soluçoes,* (São Paulo: Editora Brasiliense, 1989). The relationship between the foreign debt crisis and the exhaustion of the pattern for financing the Brazilian economy is also analyzed in Alvaro Antonia Zini, Jr., "O Brasil num Cruzamento: Dívida Externa e Exaustão Fiscal," *Revista de Economia Política* 10 (January–March 1990). For a more comprehensive analyis of the issues concerning the deficit of the public sector in Brazil, see Ernesto Lozardo, editor, *Deficit Público Brasileiro: Política Economica e Ajuste Estrutural,* (Rio de Janeiro: Editora Paz e Terra, 1987).

[9] We followed the thoughts of José Roberto Ferro, "Para Sair da Estagnaçãoe Diminuir o Atraso Tecnológico da Industria Automobílistica Brasileira," (Universidade de Campinas, 1990, Mimeographed). Besides its importance for the industrial sector's revenues, the automotive industry provides an excellent explanation of the Brazilian industrialization process. For these reasons, we thought it interesting to use this industry as an example of the exhaustion of the strategy for replacing imports, which led to the formation of Brazil's industrial complex.

[10] See Fernando Fanzylber, "Reestructuración Productiva y Competitividad: Contraste de Estrategias entre Paises Desarrollados y América Latina,"

(CEPAL/ONUDI, Reunión Grupo de Expertos de Alto Nivel sobre Estratégias y Políticas Industriales, Montevideo, 1987, Published paper).

[11] For analysis of the foreign debt crisis in the early 1980s and its impact on the Brazilian economy see, for example, Pérsio Arida, editor, *Dívida Externa, Recessão e Ajuste Estrutural—O Brasil diante da Crise* (Rio de Janeiro: Editora Paz e Terra, 1982). A historical approach to the so-called foreign debt crisis in Latin America can be found in the excellent publication *O Fim de Uma Ilusão* by Stephany Griffith-Jones and Osvaldo Sunkel (São Paulo: Editora Brasiliense).

[12] For a more thorough analysis of these points, see Gilberto Dupas and Wilson Suzigan, editors, "A Nova Articulação da Economia Mundial e as Opcões para o Brasil: Estratégia Industrial e Modernização Tecnológica," in *O Brasil e a Nova Economia Mundial* (Rio de Janeiro: José Olympio Editora, 1991).

[13] See Dupas and Suzigan, *A Nova Articulação.*

[14] The figures are mentioned in Paulo Renato de Souza, "Desafios ao Desenvolvimento Brasileiro," *Revista de Economia Política,* 10 (April–June 1990).

[15] The state of São Paulo alone, which represents approximately 45 percent of the Brazilian economy, has a domestic product above that of these three countries together.

[16] See Gilberto Dupas, "E Preciso Aprender com a Historia," in *As Perspectivas do Brasil e o Novo Governa, Forum Nacional,* edited by João Paulo dos Reis Velloso (São Paulo: Editora Nobel, 1990).

[17] See Wilson Suzigan et al., *Reestructuração Industrial e Competitividade Internacional* (Fundação SEADE, São Paulo, 1989). The importance of the definition of an industrial strategy and of state participation (respecting the signals of the market) appears mainly in the analysis of the development of Japan, South Korea, and Taiwan.

Chapter 2

Three Dimensions of the Crisis: A Political Analysis

Luciano Martins

To place the development issue in the context of the political crisis in Brazil, we must consider three distinct dimensions: (1) the Collor administration's political collapse, (2) the governance crisis, and (3) the crisis of the model of economic development. Each of these dimensions interacts with the others to produce cumulative effects, but each has a different origin and follows its own dynamics.

Collor's Political Collapse

In his inaugural address President Collor made public his government's will to introduce substantial changes in the way economic development is fostered in Brazil. Only partial and generally disjointed measures were taken, however, in part because the necessary preconditions for growth (economic stability and inflation control) had not been reached, but also because the Collor administration lacked the organized political support necessary to achieve its objectives.

Collor's lack of political support can be traced at least in part to the peculiarities of the last presidential election, in which the two candidates who reached the second round represented very small parties (each with less than 5 percent of the congressional vote); Collor's party (PRN) is a virtual fiction, created solely to allow him to present himself as a candidate. In fact, none of the existing political parties holds more than 20 percent of the congressional vote. As a consequence, government support in Congress depends either on the formation of ad hoc majorities or on the repeated use of special constitutional devices that entitle the executive to convert decisions into laws without the review of the Congress. This device was intended for very special situations, and its continual use as a substitute for Collor's lack of political support reached the limit of Congress' tolerance.

A president who cannot count on a stable congressional majority would normally attempt to forge the necessary political alliances or try to enlarge his or her political support in the first legislative election after inauguration. Strangely enough, the Collor government failed to take advantage of the first legislative election and also failed afterward in knitting new political alliances.

On the contrary, Collor moved his search for support from the domain of politics to that of propaganda and the manipulation of symbols to enhance his personal popularity. This, of course, cannot be a substitute for stable, organized political support, especially when public opinion is conditioned by hyperinflation, recession, and endless economic crisis. The results of polls on the administration's popularity clearly reflected this reality.

In short, the lack of a working majority among the parties, combined with the president's reliance on personal appeal to create political action, placed the government in a dangerous state of political isolation. This dimension of the Brazilian crisis adversely affected the policy-making process by precluding the development of consensus for addressing the nation's problems; the government could not act within the institutional framework, if it could act at all. Under more normal circumstances, the situation could have been reversed through an appropriate political alliance between the administration and its potential supporters, but in this case the ultimate result was the emergence of a new president. Much more complex is the second dimension of Brazil's present situation: the governance crisis.

The Governance Crisis

A governance crisis occurs when the state can no longer fulfill its functions, because either the decision-making process is blocked by contradictory demands or the government lacks the necessary political or material resources to enact or enforce its decisions. In short, the state as an institution (not individual administrations or leaders) becomes powerless and thus loses its ability to resolve national problems.

A governance crisis can have varied causes, can manifest itself at different loci, and can produce different outcomes, depending on the nature of the existing obstacles to the exercise of power. There are two basic types of governance crises: (1) crises that have a social origin and are related in one way or another to the existing power structure and (2) crises that are restricted to the malfunction of the political system as a result of the disorganization of state apparatuses.

The first type of crisis occurs when new social coalitions emerge that have contradictory goals and are sufficiently organized to express themselves politically but unable to prevail over their rivals. This situation gives birth to a social stalemate that tends to paralyze the state by making it unable to attend to the conflicting social or economic demands brought before it. I do not think this is the case (at least at present) in Brazil.

Brazil's governance crisis is linked, in my view, both to the financial bankruptcy of the state system and to the disorganization of its apparatuses. This is why the crisis manifests itself at two levels simultaneously. First, the available resources are insufficient to attend to systemic needs and social demands. For example, only 2 percent of the federal budget is available for investment in infrastructure. (It is important to note that this fiscal crisis cannot be explained by the imperfection of the tax system or the cost of the state bureaucracy. It is due mainly to the servicing of the national and external debt.) Second, the state apparatuses have become sites of widespread corruption or sheer disorganization. In 1990, for example, the government declared a freeze on prices in an attempt to control inflation, but no state agency was able to enforce the decision. Additonally, we can see the disastrous results created by the mismanagement of social expenditures in the social security system, basic education, and public services.

Clearly, the Brazilian state is experiencing a governance crisis of a fiscal and organizational nature, aggravated by the political troubles of the Collor administration. A continued loss of political support combined with an unsolved governance crisis could evolve in a dangerous direction. If conflicting interests within the power structure should reach a higher level or if social demands should increase faster than the resources available to satisfy them, giving rise to social upheaval, the possibility of an institutional crisis cannot be disregarded.

Yet the situation could still be managed—notwithstanding the fact that reform of the state would require a generation to resolve in light of the entrenched resistance it would have to overcome. Although the Collor government failed in three successive attempts to build a social pact to cope with the crisis, there appears to be a genuine consensus that the democratic system must be preserved.

The possibility of a crisis of power in the near future depends on curbing inflation and restoring economic growth. But even if these problems are successfully handled, one issue remains unsolved. This leads us to the third dimension to be considered: the crisis of the model of development.

The Crisis of the Model of Development

In the past fifty years, Brazil has undergone an extremely successful period of economic development—according to conventional economic indicators. There is sufficient ground to think, however, that this pattern of performance has now ended. Economic growth can still be resumed, but self-sustained economic development can no longer follow the same path.

Brazil's strategic thinking and public policies aimed at overcoming the state of underdevelopment have traditionally been influenced by the idea of nation building. Whether underdevelopment was perceived as a consequence of "economic delay" (as in the 1930s), "incomplete industrialization" (as in the 1950s), or "dependence" (as in the 1960s), as an obstacle to the construction of a "national power" (as seen in the military jargon of the 1970s), nation building was always the basic point of reference. In short, the idea of *nation* rather than *citizenship* has permeated the different *projetos de desenvolvimento*–development projects—since the 1930s.

From this conceptual matrix distinct political and ideological currents have evolved and have competed with one another for the control of the political arena. But it was the cultural framework of "national developmentalism," and the model of development derived from it, that has generally prevailed in Brazil as in other Latin American countries.

In spite of the ideological cleavages and the frequent tensions between the ideology and the public policies that were supposed to put it into effect, developmentalists shared (in deeds if not in words) a common view concerning three constituent elements of the model:

1. The need to create "national capitalism," notwithstanding the dissenting views on how autarkic it should be or what role foreign investment should play in it;
2. The need to industrialize the country by means of import substitution, despite the dissenting views concerning how extensive protectionist policies to infant industries should be; and
3. The importance of assigning to the state a fundamental role in the economic process, either as a planning agency, a financial agent, or a direct producer of goods and services—regardless of how controversial the role of the state was.

If nationalism in its different forms was the basic ideology of "national developmentalism," populism was its political support in that it allowed high economic growth coupled with minimal social tension.

The demise of this model of development can be witnessed in all the dramatic changes that took place in its constituent elements (or their milieu) during the 1980s:

- First, the idea of "national capitalism," if not the very idea of the nation-state and its correlative ideology (nationalism) faced a double challenge. On the one hand, the internationalization of production and markets created complex patterns of economic, technological, and cultural interdependence that jeopardized any attempt to achieve self-sufficient or autarkic development; on the other hand, thanks to the eruption of subregional, corporatist, and atomized social demands, nationalism seemed no longer able to create the traditional kind of social cohesion needed to attain national development goals;
- Second, the classic modes of industrialization and production organization (on which the import substitution model was based) underwent dramatic changes, thanks to what

has been called the third industrial revolution. This development has had a significant effect on the traditional comparative advantages of the developing countries (cheap labor, natural resources, and the like);

- Third, the crisis of the state and the ideological challenges to its interventionist role greatly limited its capacity to function as the main actor in the developmental process; and
- Finally, populism lost its importance as an instrument for political support and nationalistic mobilization. Classes and groups that used to be the traditional clientele of populism are now acquiring the capability to represent themselves though their own political organization.

If these four points hold, there are grounds—independent of any purely economic considerations—to think that the social and political conditions that constitute the basis for "national developmentalism" are fading out. If we consider the rising social expectations that the Brazilian development story nurtured up to 1980, it is not difficult to understand the wave of frustration and identity crisis that its possible demise is now provoking.

Brazil is passing through a period of social indecision with regard to the crisis of its model of development. This is in part because the national project that has prevailed since the 1930s is so deeply rooted in society (and has created so many vested interests) that its demise has not yet given birth to new social and political coalitions able to formulate and support an alternative project. If this is so, the possibility of protracted social and political indecision—with its paralyzing effects upon the policymaking process—cannot be disregarded. Moreover, Brazil is still learning how to deal democratically with the conflicts that arise among interest groups.

Two final points are warranted. First, if no new social and political coalitions are formed, then the neoliberal or pro–free-market approach still appears to be much more of an intellectual exercise than an actual (socially and politically rooted) alternative on which to base a new model of development.

Second, if the fiscal crisis of the state cannot be resolved and its role in the economy cannot be redefined in the short run, as I believe they will not, and if the present social indecision takes some time to dissipate and give birth to new social and political coalitions, then the short-term recipe for economic adjustment attributed to the "consensus" of the U.S. Congress,

U.S. economic agencies, and international financial institutions in Washington is rather unrealistic. To put it bluntly, the imposition of tough economic medicine as a condition for International Monetary Fund assistance or debt relief may, under the circumstances, jeopardize the painful process by which Brazil must learn to solve political and interest group conflicts through democratic procedures. The challenge of adjustment and reform cannot be permitted to threaten the consolidation of democracy.

Chapter 3

Liberalizing into Development

Amaury Porto de Oliveira

The third industrial revolution is at our door, noisily. The world of the second industrial revolution, built on a model developed in the United States and universalized under a *pax Americana*, crumbles all around us.

The theory of Kondratieff long waves (or long cycles), according to which social and political phenomena have been evolving since around 1780 in fifty-year economic cycles, can help us understand the political and economic transformation the world is undergoing. From this perspective one can argue that the industrialized economies are about to escape from the trough of a long wave (the fourth since the industrial age began in the last quarter of the eighteenth century) and enter a new phase of expansion, in the form of a third industrial revolution.

Different schools of research have explained such recurring phenomena in different ways, and I am aware that mainstream economics simply rejects the long-wave theory. Not being an economist, I am not worried about this. For some decades now, a group of serious and competent scholars have been producing a considerable body of literature on the subject.[1] I have used the theoretical insights found in this literature to structure my own observations of the contemporary world.

Throughout the second half of this century national economies have been under considerable pressure from the international community to open themselves to the international market. In this chapter I shall examine why, how, and when Brazil should yield to this pressure and proceed with the inevitable opening of its economy. It would be self-defeating to open Brazil to an unresponsive international environment. Liberalizing an economy is something to be done in a well-informed, cautious, and appropriately timed manner. The governments concerned must attempt to understand the forces now active on the world scene, busily preparing for the third industrial revolution. Particularly in countries still struggling to industrialize, the state alone will be able to promote and coordinate all the efforts necessary to address the complex problem of opening an economy.

The first section of this chapter focuses on the international and historical contexts that are conditioning all decisions on economic liberalization. The second section reviews the experiences of South Korea and Taiwan, the most successful of the "newly industrializing countries" (NICs), in adjusting their economies to these contexts. The third section deals with the weaknesses shown by Latin American countries (Brazil and Mexico, in particular) in responding to the same challenges. A final section offers some conclusions.

The Passing of "Fordism"

The four long waves that have been identified since the inception of the industrial age can be seen as two sets of two long waves each, corresponding to the first and second industrial revolutions. What distinguishes an industrial revolution is the forceful action, at its core, of social and technological patterns that together constitute the paradigm of the period. As the historical experience of the last two centuries shows, the characteristic paradigms of the two industrial revolutions have arisen from a fierce competition among evolving versions of these paradigms. Thus it was that after a protracted domestic debate the North American model of the second industrial revolution, which started under the aegis of the British model for the first revolution and occupied the whole of the third Kondratieff long wave, arose triumphantly at the end of the Second World War. The entire world came under the influence of the North American paradigm, for which the designation of "Fordism" has been gaining currency of late.[2] Fordism is a late and successful stage of capitalism characterized by large-scale production, semiskilled labor, easy credit, and mass consumption. This concept is derived from the production methods of the Ford Motor Company, particularly its use of assembly lines.

Waves naturally advance in a succession of crests and troughs, and it is fascinating to see how well the economic history of the West has adjusted to the upswings and downswings of Kondratieff long waves in the past 200 years. Particularly impressive was the turn of fortune suffered by Fordism at the onset of the 1970s. After some twenty-five years as the model for the rest of the world, Fordism suddenly plunged into the trough of the fourth Kondratieff long wave, a development that can even be symbolically dated. On August 15, 1971, President Nixon announced the U.S. unilateral decision to abandon the obligatory conversion of dollars into gold. As a result, the Bretton Woods system, which had provided the framework for extraordinary economic expansion of the 1950s and 1960s, was never the same again.

The multilateral and nondiscriminatory mechanisms created immediately after the Second World War to preside over the diffusion of the U.S. model of growth lie shattered. In their place there is a still-evolving system of administered trade characterized by the intensification of bilateral agreements for the "voluntary" restrictions of exports, the establishment of quotas and import allotments, and the arbitrary imposition of compensatory tariffs and antidumping measures. Nonindustrialized economies have found themselves increasingly segregated by this system, which is being administered for the greater profit of developed countries. From the perspective of the less developed countries, the whole exercise appears to reflect the difficulty of the erstwhile hegemon in adjusting to the erosion of its power.

This is not the place to discuss whether the United States has started its historical decline. An intense debate is under way on this theme in the United States itself, and I refer the interested reader to the relevant literature.[3] For my purposes it suffices to stress the exhaustion of the structuring value of Fordism as a model of growth. The second industrial revolution is an experience of the past. From now on, no economy can effectively grow along Fordist lines. It does not matter how relatively or absolutely robust the United States remains. Something has cracked at the core of North American society; for the United States to continue to be the leading model in the next century, it will have to bring forth a new universal paradigm.

Globalization and Regionalism: Two Trends of the Fifth Wave

As developed economies move into the fifth Kondratieff long wave, two trends are discernible in the economic organization of the world. There is a trend toward the segmentation of the international economy into very large blocs, yet at the same time observers increasingly speak of the globalization of the international economy. These two trends are not mutually exclusive because they operate at different levels of economic interaction.

Globalization is not internationalism. It is simply a manifestation of the extreme concentration of capital and technological capacity in the hands of a shrinking number of very large firms with transnational reach. Contrary to the expectations of those internationalist spirits who hope for a "single world," globalization has been growing to the detriment of vast contingents of the global population. Hundreds of millions of people find themselves left out of technological progress, and many of them experienced declining material and spiritual living conditions.

Globalization is characterized by continuous flows of people, goods and services, and capital and information, and it is not uncommon for such flows to cross over the boundaries of nation-states. Conflicts can and do emerge between the logic of globalization and the specific interests and obligations of states, even when states shelter the agents of globalization. Out of this conflict of interests arises the second trend—the segmentation of the world into coherent economic blocs, or regionalism. Globalization obeys the logic of profit and the efficient allocation of resources. Regionalism responds to the logic of governments that must tend to the best interests of their citizens.

Three large coherent blocs are now taking shape within the international economy: unified Europe, the U.S.-Canada-Mexico free trade area, and a group of Pacific-rim countries. Usually they are presented as the prefiguration of commercial megablocs, closed to third parties. Such an evolution, full of threatening consequences for countries like Brazil, must be resisted forcefully. But I do not think the partition of the world into discriminatory megablocs would be fatal. Developed countries have no interest in going back to the trade wars of the 1930s.

It seems more correct, and more stimulating, to consider the emergence of these blocs as an expression of the ongoing competition among candidates for leadership in the third industrial revolution. I suggest that we look to these blocs, then, as laboratories of paradigmatic experimentation, rather than as the embryos of megablocs.

EVOLVING PARADIGMS

Three countries are clearly engaged in competition for leadership in the third industrial revolution, each as the dynamic nucleus of its respective region: the United States, Japan, and Germany. The status of Japan and Germany as the first examples in history of a new type of international economic, nonmilitary power allows us to predict a new era of international relations in which the dynamic factor will no longer be political-military but economic and social.[4]

In a recent article two professors from Centre d'Etudes Prospectives et d'Informations Internationales in Paris offered a quantified and up-to-date comparison of these three laboratories of paradigmatic experimentation at the present stage of their competition.[5] Gérard Lafay and Colette Herzog consider their subject from the point of view of competitiveness in high-technology exports, a category that covers electronics; motors, turbines, and pumps; heavy electrical materials; aeronautics; pharmaceuticals; and plastics and fibers. Their study covers the seven most developed countries of the Organization for Economic Cooperation and Development (OECD) and the four East Asian NICs: South Korea, Taiwan, Singapore, and Hong Kong.

Lafay and Herzog first tried to determine the difference between exports and imports, or relative balance, in each country's aggregate high-technology trade. In 1967, the first year analyzed, the United States had a relative balance equivalent to 17 percent of the world trade in high-technology products. What was then West Germany appeared in a distant second place, with 9 percent of the world trade. Japan and the United Kingdom competed for third place, with about 3 percent. The East Asian NICs had negative balances.

Twenty years later the situation had been reversed. In 1988, the last year covered by the study, the U.S. relative balance between exports and imports of high-technology products had reached equilibrium after being negative in 1986 and 1987. The West German balance continued to be positive but fell to

3 percent. Japan, conversely, had jumped ahead to first place, with a balance equivalent to 14 percent of the world trade. Equally impressive was the performance of the four Asian NICs, which together presented a positive balance of 2 percent of the world's high-technology trade—putting them in third place, behind only Japan and West Germany.

Lafay and Herzog then looked for the relative balance presented by the same countries, during the same period, in their aggregate trade of manufactures in general. Again, first place went to Japan, with 7 percent of the world trade of manufactures in 1988, as against 4.5 percent in 1967. West Germany fell from first place in 1967 (7 percent) to second (5 percent) in 1988. Again, the four Asian NICs performed well, rising to third place in 1988 (2 percent relative balance) in comparison with a negative position (−0.5 percent) in 1967. The United States, never a good performer in the world trade of manufactures in general, merely managed in 1988 to reach an equilibrium in imports and exports, after a negative relative balance (−8 percent) in 1986.

Finally, to fine-tune the image obtained in the two previous analyses, Lafay and Herzog measured the proportion of high-technology products in the relative balance of manufactures in general. Here, the United States regained its brilliance, maintaining first place with high-technology products contributing 14 percent to the U.S. relative balance for manufactures in 1988. This was an extraordinary performance, even though it represented a gradual erosion in the previously indisputable U.S. supremacy. In 1970, the best year for U.S. high-technology exports, their part in the U.S. relative balance for manufactures amounted to 21 percent. West Germany was also losing momentum: the contribution of high-technology products to its relative balance for manufactures, positive until 1970, was negative (−3 percent) in 1988. Japan was marching in the opposite direction: from a negative position until 1974, through a steady ascension ever since Japan reached the U.S. level (14 percent) in 1988. Also, the Asian NICs gained a lot of ground: from −16 percent in 1967 to −4 percent in 1988, almost equivalent to the German position.

The findings of Lafay and Herzog lead to three main inferences. First, the United States shows persistent vigor on the technological frontier. Although, as we have seen, the structuring value of Fordism has been exhausted, the United States is still capable of supplying the model for the third industrial revolution. Japan is certainly a major competitor for such a position. Although Japan has already produced an impressive array of paradigmatic innovations, however, it is still premature to speak of a Japanese model for the third industrial revolution.[6]

Second, Japan's trajectory has been extraordinary and deserves to be studied by countries in Brazil's position. The findings of Lafay and Herzog reveal an inflection in Japan's economic evolution around 1974, a striking coincidence in timing with the plunge of Fordism into the trough of the fourth Kondratieff long wave. This is worth looking into through a review of the energy crises of the 1970s.

After its defeat in World War II Japan was led by the U.S. occupation authorities to reindustrialize according to the triumphant U.S. model, with its characteristic reliance on oil. Tokyo was made to abandon its traditional governmental control of the energy base of the Japanese economy, opening the way for the dominance of Anglo-Saxon oil companies. Japan's dependency on imported energy jumped from 24 percent in 1955 to 90 percent in 1973. Oil came to represent 77 percent of energy imports. In late 1973, when oil prices quadrupled and the oil companies notified the government of a forced reduction in supply, the Japanese public grew alarmed for the future of the country. Suddenly aware of its backwardness as compared to the countries at the forefront of the second industrial revolution, with their patrimony of knowledge and experience, Japan decided to overhaul the way in which it had been promoting economic growth.[7]

As we examine this decision more closely, we will be able to observe the historical phenomenon of paradigms at work. Long-wave theorists borrowed the notion of a central paradigm for an identified economic formation from the work of Thomas S. Kuhn on the history of science.[8] Kuhn used the idea of a scientific paradigm to identify the outlook, the model, and the pattern that would preside over the attitudes of scientists in their research and subsequent conclusions during a certain epoch. Long-wave theorists speak of a technological paradigm or, more comprehensively, of a socioeconomic paradigm to identify different segments of the historical evolution of socioeconomic life.

I view paradigms, either in a dominant position or in competition with other possible versions, as the mediating patterns that transform long waves from a mere series of statistical averages into an established segment of historical reality, or, taking inspiration from Giovanni Dosi, as the pattern of problem solving an economy adopts to drive onward.[9] Examined in this light, Japan's trajectory of modernization provides an excellent exemplar for societies intent on catching up with developed countries. This is the third inference to be drawn from the French study.

In the second half of the nineteenth century American steamships forced open the self-contained society that had matured in Japan under 300 years of shogunate dominance. Thereafter, the manufactures of the West, and Great Britain, the leading economy of the first industrial revolution, easily occupied some of the most important Japanese markets, such as cotton textiles. But whereas the other Asian countries that faced Western pressures for an "open door" soon fell into semi-colonial status, Japan escaped through the clear-sighted, cautious, and well-timed way in which both state and society reacted to the intrusions of industrialized countries. Japan thus provided the first example of what I would characterize as liberalization into development.

Central to Japan's success was the realization by its government and intelligensia of the importance of modern technology. Convinced that Japan could not survive as an independent country without creatively absorbing the Western technology of the day, government, intellectuals, and business joined forces to put Japan on the road to a late industrialization.

By the end of the ninteenth century that road was being followed by, among others, the United States and Germany, which were to become the main contenders for leadership in the second industrial revolution. Japan was not able to reach quite the same level of excellence as the Western late industrializers of that time. But with the benefit of hindsight it now becomes possible to trace the origins, at least in part, of the exceptional success of Japan's second attempt at late industrialization to the very weakness of her previous experiment.

According to Ichizo Yamauchi, an industrial analyst with the Nomura Research Institute, economic modernization in Japan before the Second World War took on a dual character.[10] Government and the private sector were united by the national goal of building a domestic technology production system by modifying imported technology. Two different purposes had to be served, however. The first purpose was to provide first-class technological products for defense-related activities—without concern for cost. As defense production came to dominate the Japanese machine industry before the war, however, government and industrialists were diverted from the aim of adapting foreign technology for the production of first-class equipment with available Japanese resources.

The second purpose was to strengthen the competitiveness of nondefense industries vis-à-vis overseas companies in both domestic and overseas markets. Nondefense industries were preoccupied with reducing their production costs by substituting cheap, domestically produced equipment for expensive imported equipment. Also, they had to contend with technologies developed for societies in which the proportion of skilled male workers in the total labor force was already as high as 40 percent. Notwithstanding the introduction of an efficient and compulsory system of popular education, the proportion of skilled male workers among total employees in Japan could not realistically be higher than 15 percent. All this meant that the mass production of standardized manufactures, the very essence of the U.S. model of the second industrial revolution, remained unsatisfactorily developed in Japan in the period prior to World War II.

After the war, when Japan was reindustrialized under the aegis of the U.S. army, excellence in mass production methods became the top priority of the authorities and companies concerned with industrialization. The accumulated knowledge of the old defense industries was of great help to the government and firms evaluating the potential and importance of the new sectors, such as electronics, whose technologies had been developed during the war and which the United States was now transferring to civilian use. Japan's ability to take a strategic approach to industrial production and the commercialization of its products was coupled with an urgent need to acquire expertise in mass production. In this endeavor it had all the advantages of a follower. That is, it could learn from the errors and hesitations of the initiator—and learn the best possible lessons.

By the mid-1970s, Japan had almost caught up with the leading industrialized countries. With the shock of the sudden rise in oil prices, Japan was faced with the challenge of transforming itself from follower to at least an associate in world leadership.

Some fifteen years later, authors such as Alain Lipietz argue that Japan did not simply catch up with the United States but overtook it by discovering a new, post-Fordist way of converting manual and intellectual skill into increased productivity. As two U.S. professors contend: "Japanese industrial organization has reached a level of development that is post-Fordist. This replaces the specialization and deskilling of the Fordist model with a new industrial organization based upon integrative and flexible work organization, shopfloor learning, and networked production complexes."[11]

The East Asian NICs Adjust to the New Economic Order

It is impossible to judge the correctness of and opportunity for economic liberalization in the second half of the twentieth century unless the decisions taken toward that end are seen in the double context provided by the international march of Fordism and the demands of U.S. hegemony. As Robert Gilpin explains, periods of hegemonic stability are characterized by the installation, by dint and benevolence of the hegemon, of an open and liberal world economy.[12] The thriving hegemonic power establishes and maintains the norms and rules of a liberal economic order; when the hegemon declines, the liberal economic order is greatly weakened.

The role of the hegemonic power, adds Gilpin, is to

> serve as an example of the benefits of the market system and perform as an engine of growth for the rest of the system; its imports stimulate the growth of other economies and its investments provide developing countries with the financing needed for growth. The process of technology transfer and knowledge diffusion also supplies developing economies with the technology and technical expertise required for their industrialization and economic development. This role of the hegemon in the global process of economic growth is a cement that helps hold the system together; when this growth declines, centrifugal forces increasingly manifest themselves.[13]

Such a role was performed by the United States under the system of the *pax Americana*—but with an important reservation. The onset of the cold war limited the area of U.S. interest and conditioned its disposition to promote economic progress. The United States provided effective assistance only to those nations whose advancement would help contain the spread of communism. This preoccupation accounts for the different treatment Washington has bestowed upon East Asian and Latin American NICs.

The concept of newly industrialized countries (NICs) was created in the 1960s and 1970s to designate economies in which the strategies of import substitution industrialization (ISI) had ceased being primary (or horizontal) and became secondary (or vertical). In horizontal ISI the first steps are taken toward industrialization: the processing of primary products and the production of nondurable consumer goods that are no longer imported. In vertical ISI the production of intermediate goods (such as petrochemicals or steel), along with capital goods (such as machines) and durable consumer goods (such as cars and refrigerators), is initiated. In secondary ISI the technological complexity of the production process increases, and the industrial structure becomes vertical, leading to the introduction of heavy industry.[14]

The countries that became NICs followed different paths. To illustrate how economies already halfway to industrialization differ in their opening to the external world, I focus in this section on two East Asian NICs, South Korea and Taiwan, and in the following section on two Latin American countries, Brazil and Mexico.

The histories of South Korea and Taiwan are tied to the installation of the *pax Americana* on the Pacific rim of Asia.[15] Faced with the communist victory in China and the spreading threat of guerrilla movements in the European colonies of Southeast Asia, the United States reversed course in Japan. During the first years of its military occupation, the United States had adopted the policy of dissolving Japan's prewar structures. At the outset of the 1950s, the United States abandoned that plan, deciding instead to create a Japan–East Asia sphere of commerce. Washington thus began exerting considerable political influence, and investing substantial economic and military aid, in order to transform Japan into the "natural workshop of the East," neatly complemented by the Southeast Asian countries, which were given the function of supplying Japan with raw materials for food and industry. Taiwan and South Korea, as territorial entities artificially delimited by the cold war itself, were left out of this sphere of commerce. Treated as bulwarks of U.S. strategic defense in the North Pacific, these prospective NICs instead joined the community of nations and the capitalist order of the second industrial revolution in close association with the evolution of U.S. strategies.

Between 1951 and 1965 the United States provided $3.7 billion to Taiwan and another $4 billion to South Korea for military aid, general economic assistance, training and education programs, investments in road and port infrastructure, and the creation of public services. From 1947 to 1950 in South Korea and from 1949 to 1953 in Taiwan the United States encouraged the development of an agrarian reform program and provided both technical and financial assistance in its implementation. In Taiwan the U.S. Congress created the Sino-American Joint Commission on Rural Reconstruction (JCRR), a special organ that acted as Taiwan's de facto Ministry for Agriculture until 1979. In addition to implementing agrarian reform the JCRR financed more than half the formation of liquid capital in Taiwanese agriculture, thereby helping to create one of the fundamental conditions for the subsequent industrialization of the island.[16]

Apart from U.S. strategic demands, Seoul and Taipei were constantly aware of the concrete threats from the rival regimes of Pyongyang and Beijing. Thus it was that in 1969, when the Nixon Doctrine formalized Washington's policy of encouraging regional defense cooperation among third-world countries as a prelude to making them more responsible for their own defense, South Korea and Taiwan both launched comparable efforts to obtain military self-reliance. Washington was particularly responsive. The Nixon Doctrine had liberalized the rules for the export of arms and military technology, providing far greater access to sophisticated U.S. technology than ever before. South Korea and Taiwan received privileged treatment, becoming the only countries outside NATO and Western Europe to be awarded coproduction contracts with the United States for significant combat equipment.[17]

To build military self-reliance, South Korea and Taiwan needed to acquire a satisfactory level of industrial precision and quality through a highly qualified and specialized work force. A few precision industries were established, and the whole process converged to the enhancement of the two countries' industrial capacity. U.S. support and assistance to its two allies put South Korea and Taiwan on the path of late industrialization. From then on it was up to them to assimilate and develop, in accordance with local conditions, the modernizing elements that Fordism had been diffusing worldwide.

A critical element in the development of both countries was the pattern by which they progressed. Since the early 1960s Taiwan and South Korea had moved from their initial experimentation with horizontal ISI directly into the first stage of an outward-oriented industrial development (OID1), during which industrializing countries try to export labor-intensive manufactures. This choice of an outward-oriented growth strategy was not only pressed by U.S. advisers but also made possible by the opening of the U.S. market to East Asian manufactures.[18] During the 1960s East Asia became a preferred location for U.S. firms looking for cheap offshore production to compensate for loss of competitiveness in the U.S. domestic market. Subcontracting, outsourcing, and similar practices prevailed among U.S. producers or distributors and the incipient exporters of South Korea and Taiwan. The subsequent extraordinary growth of East Asian NICs would not have been possible without this opening of the U.S. domestic market.

Latin American NICs, as we shall see, passed from horizontal to vertical ISI, not benefiting from the sustained gains in competitiveness brought by active participation in international trade. This path of development was not only an expression of the entrenched resistance to change that the United States had never helped to break in Latin America; it was also the result of the traditional U.S. view of Latin America as a source of raw materials for U.S. industries and a market for U.S. manufacturers, a relationship driven by the U.S. private sector.

It has become usual for free-market economists and politicians to equate outward-oriented growth strategies with reliance on market forces and price signals and to establish an idealized antithesis between the supposed market liberalization wisely adopted by East Asian NICs and the crippling intervention and inward-oriented approaches identified with Latin America. In reality the connections between strategy, policies, and politics are much more mixed than those theories imply, and a growing and serious literature has made clear that a public-policy commitment to export-oriented growth is the key to achieving global status as an exporter of manufactures. As stated by Colin Bradford, at the root of the East Asian NICs' success is a national commitment to integrating diverse policy instruments into a coherent strategy.[19]

When South Korea and Taiwan switched from ISI to OID1 in the early 1960s, both countries adopted policy packages aimed at export promotion: reforms in exchange-rate systems, measures to liberalize import restrictions, and a system of export incentives. This approach contributed to the rapid expansion of the two countries' exports in the open and market-oriented economy of the non-communist world. But it was the ability of the South Korean and Taiwanese governments to use export growth as the impetus for an interactive process of capital accumulation and technological progress—to ensure that liberalization was put at the service of development—that really led them onto a path of sustained growth.

The guiding hand of the state became more visible in both South Korea and Taiwan when, in the early 1970s, the two countries began to diversify into the second stage of an outward-oriented industrial development (OID2), characterized by the increased exportation of capital- and technology-intensive products. They soon moved into an OID2 complex, defined by Edward K. Y. Chen as "a stage in which import substitution of capital and intermediate products (secondary import substitution) occurs simultaneously with export orientation. Sectors providing financial, technical, and other professional services may grow concomitantly."[20]

South Korea and Taiwan had by then become Japanese-style developing countries, with the responsibility of implementing the OID2 complex.[21] Showing great proficiency and understanding of the way in which modern economies work, the two developing states were able to navigate between ISI and OID, working through the market and for the market, but always mindful of the national goal of full industrialization.

Avoiding foreign direct investment as much as possible, and never giving up the potential for international competitiveness created by OID, the two East Asian NICs did not refrain from reintroducing protective policies typical of ISI as they diversified into heavy and chemical industrialization. They instituted measures for industry protection and market controls for iron and steel, petrochemicals, oil refining, shipbuilding, machinery production, electronics, and cement. Simultaneously, the two countries created fiscal and financial incentives to attract private domestic capital to these sectors and established consistent policies for the import and development of appropriate technology and human capital.

During the 1960s and 1970s the liberalization measures undertaken by these countries were mostly token gestures, and a series of hidden restrictions limited the flow of imports. They mainly sought to expose their own exports to international competition so that they could become competitive in their own right. It was only in the early 1980s that the two East Asian NICs, mainly yielding to pressure from the United States, decided to open their domestic markets to international competition, with both Seoul and Taipei announcing plans to reach the level of import liberalization rates and tariff rates of the OECD countries by 1992. Both countries are also preparing to join the club of industrialized countries by the turn of the century.[22]

Taiwan and South Korea are two fine examples, perhaps the only complete examples to date, of third-world economies that have approached the level of development of the industrialized countries. They have reaped as they have sowed, with liberalization policies that have been well-informed, cautious, and appropriately timed. It is true, however, that both Taiwan and South Korea benefited from extremely favorable international circumstances (as long as neither actually competed with the industrialized economies), and this poses the crucial question to Brazil: Is it still possible to enter into a late industrialization process at this stage in the deterioration of a liberal world economy installed fifty years ago by the now-declining U.S. hegemon?

Latin America Stays Behind

The Bretton Woods system, the financial mainstay of the *pax Americana*, resulted from a laborious compromise between the ideas of John Maynard Keynes and ideas largely inspired by Cordell Hull, a disciple of Woodrow Wilson and for a long period Franklin D. Roosevelt's secretary of state. This compromise, achieved during the protracted "Washington Negotiations" (1941–1946), was characterized to an excessive degree by the desire to prevent a repetition of the conflict-filled 1930s, a period of serious tension among the industrialized countries. This led to a permanent cleavage between "advanced" countries, which established the new system, and those "in development," which were left to accept the agreements of the wealthier nations.

When the world was rebuilt after World War II, Latin America was left unaided. The continent received neither Marshall Plan aid nor special attention from the U.S. hegemon. Promises were made but routinely broken. With regard to the restructuring of international trade, for example, a charter reflecting some of the liberal ideas of Cordell Hull was signed in Havana, in 1948, but it was never ratified by the U.S. Congress. This charter created the International Trade Organization, an institution for which Latin American countries had ardently fought; neglected by Congress, it fell into oblivion and was "provisionally" replaced by the General Agreement on Tariffs and Trade (GATT) regime. Similarly, in the "Point Four" program of his inaugural address President Truman promised to use U.S. "technical knowledge" to help resolve the underdevelopment of Latin America, Africa, and Asia, but this assistance never materialized. When Truman presented his first state of the union address one year later, it had become clear that Point Four had lost its edge as an instrument for the reconstruction of the undeveloped areas in general. Point Four, the president stressed, was needed "particularly in the Far East."[23]

The reason for this narrowed focus was, of course, the incipient construction of one of the main lines of defense in the "containment of communism" along Asia's Pacific rim. Containing communism was also a preoccupation of the hegemon in Latin America, but the matter had already been dealt with, under the rubric of "hemispheric defense," by the Rio Pact of 1947, which required collective action by the American states if any one of them came under attack.

Latin America's segregation from the mainstream of international development has a long history. The countries of the region were left to their own devices during the international depression that begain in 1929. In the 1930s they reacted to the situation by instituting policies of industrialization by the substitution of imports (ISI). Latin American ISI was mainly financed by domestic capital, transferred from the agriculture and mining sectors' economic surplus to industry. The base of support came from a broad industrializing coalition comprising the state, domestic industrialists, middle sectors (both civilian and military), and segments of the social sectors. The deep-rooted conservatism of such coalitions, acutely manifest in their incapacity to face the crucial issue of agrarian reform, acted as a brake to the expansion of internal markets, which were supposed to provide the base for Latin American industrialization.[24]

In contrast to its policy in East Asia under the *pax Americana*, the United States did not help Latin American countries overcome the structural barriers to agrarian reform, one of the main preconditions to the onset of industrialization, as shown more than 200 years ago in England and France. In the post–World War II era, U.S. interest in effectively drawing Japan, South Korea, and Taiwan into the international liberal economy led Washington to participate actively in the implementation of policies that proved beneficial both to the hegemon and to the concerned country. To the United States, it was important, for instance, to create in these countries a strong group of middle-class landowners to provide an efficient bulwark against leftist movements and to keep conservative parties in power.

But South Korea and Taiwan also benefited from the modernization of the countryside. Rural productivity increased, creating the conditions for increased savings and the expansion of the domestic market. Local industries were favored by cheaper supplies of raw materials and an inflow of laborers, drawn from an excess supply then available in the agriculture sector. The economic system became more equitable, and last but not least, the old anti-industrializing elites could be squeezed out of power. Late industrialization cannot succeed unless the industrializing state has the ability to insulate itself from rent-seeking entrepreneurs, which is possible only if a new class of risk-taking capitalists free from ties with the obsolescent rural structures comes to the fore.

I am touching here on one of the most controversial points in the history of U.S. relations with Latin America, namely, whether or not the United States is interested in promoting the economic and political progress of the nations south of the Rio Grande. The issue has produced an extensive literature, which was particularly abundant during and after the 1960s, the decade of the Alliance for Progress. This initiative, proclaimed by President Kennedy in 1961, was the most ambitious and comprehensive manifestation of Washington's determination to help Latin America, and it is melancholy to read the conclusion reached in 1969 by the respected Republican U.S. senator, Henry Cabot Lodge: "The total effect of the Alliance has been to solidify the status quo, to entrench the oligarchy, and to heighten the obstacles to change."[25]

This is not the place to dwell on such controversy. What I wish to stress is that under the *pax Americana* the hegemonic power behaved differently with regard to East Asian and Latin American NICs, guiding itself almost exclusively by strategic considerations regarding the containment of communism. This had profound developmental consequences for the four countries I have been examining (South Korea and Taiwan; Brazil and Mexico).

The disparate treatment that the United States accorded the various NICs resulted in asymmetries in the geographical pattern of U.S. trade. For example, as William H. Branson has shown:

> In overall trade in manufactures, the United States has a large surplus ($12.2 billion in 1980) in trade with the Latin American NICs (Argentina, Brazil, Colombia, Mexico), a small surplus ($2.5 billion) with the ASEAN (Association of South East-Asian Nations) countries, and a large deficit ($11.3 billion) with the Far Eastern NICs (Hong Kong, South Korea, Taiwan). Thus the United States exports capital goods to the NICs and imports consumer goods from them, following broad lines of comparative advantage. But the exports are relatively focused on Latin America, mainly Mexico, and imports on the Far Eastern NICs. . . . [A] trade triangle appears, with the United States exporting manufactures, mainly capital goods, to the Latin American NICs; who in turn sell raw materials on the world market. The Far Eastern NICs buy raw materials and sell manufactures, mainly consumer goods, to the United States.[26]

All things considered, it is no surprise that Brazil and Mexico, the two Latin American countries that were the most successful in promoting horizontal ISI, proved so inefficient when in the 1950s they were faced with the need to widen and verticalize their industrial bases. Restrained by a colossal lack of information on the real state of the world and the forces at play outside their countries' borders, which is characteristic of

Latin American elites, the industrializing coalitions in Brazil and Mexico were not able by themselves to make the jump into OID1, as preparation for OID2. Obsessed with the many rents that could be captured in the domestic market, Brazilian and Mexican industrialists shunned a positive effort of entry into the international market when Fordism was still expanding.

Neither could the state, which even in a nationalistic Latin America was never as determined and proficient as the developing states of East Asia, ameliorate the timorous behavior of the industrialists. Instead of adopting judicious policies of human capital formation and the wise development of a domestic technological base, Brazil and Mexico opted for the indiscriminate importation of technology under the preposterous supposition that this would lead directly into "modernity," dispensing with the worrisome expenses and efforts of apprenticeship.[27]

The result has become known in Brazil as the "triple alliance," a combination of forces in which the state absorbed the effort of investment in infrastructure and heavy industry; private Brazilian capitalists continued to deal with traditional ISI industries; and foreign direct investment (FDI) was called in to support new sectors requiring the importation of technology, as in the case of the automotive industry, chosen to become the mainstay of Brazil's vertical ISI.[28]

In sum, Brazil and Mexico decided to solve a perceived local scarcity of capital and technology by bringing in transnational companies and entrusting them to raise the technological level of their countries in the new industrial sectors, with the important exception of energy. In the early 1970s, as shown by studies of the time, 50 percent of the roughly 300 largest manufacturing firms in Brazil and Mexico were under foreign control. In the more dynamic sectors, such as the chemical industry or the production of transport equipment, that proportion was even larger.

The costs and benefits of relying on transnational companies to enhance the technological base of the economy is another controversial issue in Brazil. Professor Werner Baer has made a balanced presentation of the debate surrounding that subject. I will deal exclusively with the effects these companies had on economic liberalization.[29]

Two key aspects must be emphasized in this discussion. First, contrary to the situation in East Asia (Japan and NICs), the transnationals reinforced and profited from the Latin American trend of protecting the domestic market against certain imports. Protectionist policies were also employed in East Asia, but there, in the framework of OID2, they were intended to favor national firms in the acquisition and absorption of imported technology, whereas in Latin America, in the framework of vertical ISI, they were extended indiscriminately to final products. A very liberal import regime favored precisely those capital goods and intermediate products that incorporated most of the technologies being transferred. The transnationals were thus the main beneficiaries of this policy. It is seldom recognized that "inward-oriented industrialization" under the *pax Americana* worked very much in favor of transnational capital.

Second, there was a preponderance of transnational companies in the more dynamic sectors of the protected Latin American economy. By the second half of the 1960s, when the Latin American governments belatedly recognized that sustained economic development would depend on their ability to compete in international markets, they were soon confronted not only with the neoprotectionism of the industrialized countries but also with the need to conduct their export drive through incentives and favors to foreign firms. By 1969, for example, one of every three foreign subsidiaries in Brazil was participating in the export drive. These subsidiaries accounted for 43 percent of the country's overall exports that year. The proportion of machinery and vehicles reached 75 percent.[30]

Since no real absorption of technology occurred in the modern economic sectors of Latin America, and since effective human resource policies were not implemented to sustain export performance through improved competitiveness, the export promotion policies of the late 1960s and the 1970s led to aggressive credit and exchange policies. In country after country south of the Rio Grande export drives became bogged down in a tangle of spurious competitiveness, which in fact contributed to the growing trend toward economic globalization for the greater benefit of transnational firms.

Notwithstanding all the weaknesses and contradictions typical of Latin American countries, and lack of constructive stimulus from the current hegemon, by the late 1960s Brazil and

Mexico, primarily on the strength of their performance as exporters of manufactures, were being internationally accepted as NICs, with a level of attainment equivalent to the East Asian NICs. By the end of the 1970s, as the effects of the downswing in the fourth Kondratieff long wave became widespread, however, important differences had begun to emerge in the capacity of the various NICs to react to the adversities of international life.

South Korea and Taiwan, for instance, showed a better capacity to adjust to the monetary disturbances occasioned by the two leaps in oil prices in the 1970s, thus escaping from the debt trap that was to immobilize Latin America during the 1970s. It is important, however, not to reduce the explanation of such a difference in results to the simple allegation that the East Asian economies liberalized more than the Latin American economies.

Rather, it is necessary to consider the international and historical context of economic liberalization in these countries since World War II. One must consider the proficiency and the correctness of timing demonstrated by each liberalizing government; and finally, one must review the objectives of the liberalizing measures. The question that subsumes all these considerations, and through which we can judge the success of economic liberalization, is, How close to the contemporary technological frontier did the economy come after opening up to the international market?

It is by this standard that we can best evaluate the success of South Korea and Taiwan in the 1980s as Brazil and Mexico stagnated. Because the two East Asian NICs were able to widen their cautious, well-timed, and well-informed liberalization policies during that decade while the two Latin American NICs remained entangled in their own barriers to progress and neglected by the external world, two very different outcomes have naturally emerged. But there is a further point to be made: the two sets of governments demonstrated differences in their ability to grasp the changes in the external world.

In my opinion, what fundamentally distinguished the East Asian cases from those of the Latin American NICs in the fateful decade of the 1980s was their ability to perceive the imminent paradigmatic shift in the industrialized world. The East Asians saw that the second industrial revolution was coming to its end and presciently began cutting their links with Fordism. This has yet to be done in Latin America.

This fact demands redoubled prudence against calls to replicate the experience of the East Asian NICs in Latin America. It is impractical now to attempt to repeat the successes of previous decades. To become a late industrializer, Latin America must look into the future.[31]

What Can Be Done?

Some authors consider the present moment in history as a period of transition from a network of national economies, interconnected in space and time, to a so-called "world economy," defined as a unique aggregate of regions and phenomena, distinct one from the other but totally interdependent. Latin American economies will be ineluctably carried along by the force of this transition. It is important to be aware that during this period the earlier links within the network of Latin America's national economies will be loosened, providing for some time to come the flexibility needed to create new relationships with the external world.

This transitional period of flexibility makes it possible to imagine, for a few years more, the emergence of bold and innovative associations that take advantage of the present trend toward regionalism. Essentially, this trend expresses the need for countries marked by some sort of proximity—geographical, historical, cultural, or economic—to unite to better defend the legitimate aspirations of their populations. As we have seen, three major laboratories of paradigmatic experimentation are presently being organized along regional lines. But there is space for smaller regional associations, even inside the area of the megaspaces. And it is here that the Latin American countries should find their best opportunities for growth.

Latin American countries have found themselves limited to two traditional links with the international economy: Latin America–United States and Latin America–Europe. But we must not forget the presence of a third powerhouse: East Asia. This region comprises countries like South Korea and Taiwan, which are still at a stage of development compatible with the technological capabilities and needs of a country such as Brazil. Latin American countries, which are presently in a state of perplexity about how to be accepted in areas that are excluding them, would perhaps do better to begin disassociating themselves from the old ties.

In the so-called Southern Cone of Latin America, the governments of four countries marked by many similarities (Argentina, Brazil, Paraguay, and Uruguay) have already entered into a regional association known as MERCOSUR. This is a development full of promise, provided the association continues to operate in a spirit of "open regionalism"—that is, to mediate between the old vertical ties and new, innovative horizontal relationships.

If designed and implemented as a tool for the construction of a multilateralist world economy, not as a potential component of some megabloc, MERCOSUR can add dynamism to its members' economies within the globalist-regionalist framework. MERCOSUR will make the unavoidable economic reforms to be tackled by the member economies more palatable and will provide more bargaining power for the group in its relations with the leaders of the paradigmatic laboratories.

Given the current redistribution of global economic power, for instance, one can anticipate that countries expecting to lead the third industrial revolution will attach great importance to direct access to both the Pacific and Atlantic market expansions. The United States has an advantage over Japan in this respect. But the Japanese deficiency could be overcome to a certain extent through more intensive economic and technological cooperation between Japan and MERCOSUR. In the post–cold war world the weakening of the ideological straightjacket works both ways. The United States need no longer feel so obliged to prevent Latin American countries from falling to communism; Latin America need no longer feel constrained to limit its technological improvement in the name of a now-rhetorical goal of "continental defense."

At such a historical moment and within such an international context, how can a developing economy successfully open itself to the international market? Is there still any hope for economies that have let the favorable upswing of the fourth Kondratieff long wave pass them by?

I am optimistic, basing my conclusions on thought-provoking articles by Francisco R. Sagasti (1989)[32] and a team of researchers writing in *Revista de la CEPAL* (August 1991).[33] According to

Sagasti, Latin America is facing a critical situation in which it is likely to remain entangled for the rest of the century if it does not begin to act as a kind of "social laboratory," and to generate new, broad-based solutions. He emphasizes five areas that demand innovative treatment: social inequities, productive homogeneity, the shortage of financial resources, obsolescence in scientific and technological capacity, and segregation from the international community, including inadequate openness of Latin American economies to the international market. The central factor in solving the final problem is Latin America's flexibility, as previously mentioned, which may, at this moment in history, bring the region out of its quandary.

Sagasti, writing in 1988, does not provide concrete suggestions on how to use Latin America's temporary flexibility. He is content to urge the region to take advantage of the relative relaxation in its traditional ties to the international economy before new patterns of economic interaction begin to crystallize at the end of the 1990s. It now seems possible to be more precise. For the Southern Cone countries MERCOSUR seems to offer a feasible and promising route to development, particularly if it is undertaken as an experiment in "open regionalism" and as a regional association that feels free to develop a nexus with the dynamic group of East Asian NICs.

Southern Cone countries exhibit strong structural heterogeneity. As Sagasti stresses, there are differences among the livestock-agricultural, industrial, mineral, and services sectors, as well as among the production units within these sectors. To correct this situation, Sagasti advises that the countries of the region begin by identifying categories of relatively homogeneous units in the production of goods and services and then draw up specific policies for the use of technology in these production units. Each sector can then receive more appropriate technological assistance, whether in the form of technological research, quality control, productivity improvement, or the formation of links with international centers of excellence. Such an approach offers MERCOSUR a comprehensive program that can be implemented through the common effort of the government and business sectors with the creative mediation of the academic community.

Some innovative academic insights can be found in the *Revista de la CEPAL* article, which synthesizes some very recent research by economists who are interested in economic development problems and share a desire to find ways to reactivate Latin America's growth after the "lost decade" of the 1980s. For example, the appropriate course to follow in the quest for international competitiveness, which is considered the fundamental factor in any serious effort to modernize an economy, is being newly debated. Under discussion is the question of whether it would be better to start by reforming the internal structure of the economy or to reformulate the commercial policies of the country in order to provoke responses from the national economy to external demand.

The researchers mentioned in the *Revista* article tend to prefer internally generated growth to the traditional view of export-led growth as the appropriate soil for the germination of export dynamism. They concede that no economy can become competitive without concern for international prices or access to external technology through trade. An open economy is necessary. But they emphasize that attention to exports and the commercial reforms necessary to promote them is only one side of the problem. One must never forget that the conceptual admissibility and practical effectiveness of a growth strategy draw legitimacy and strength from the dynamism and competitiveness of the national economy.

All things considered, then, what can be done to insert Brazil into the interdependent "world economy" of the 1990s, at a time when free trade may well be more important to smaller, dynamic economies than to the hegemonic leader of the international liberal economy of the post–World War II era? The so-called "liberal revolution" that is supposed to be leading Latin America toward modernization, with Mexico as the prime example, does not meet the criterion established in this chapter: that the success of economic liberalization must be defined by how near an economy comes to the contemporary technological frontier after opening up to the international market.

Judged by this standard, it is sad to see Mexico reduced to a level of industrialization equivalent to that of Malaysia, when twenty years ago Mexico was being compared to South Korea. Now many South Korean firms are following the example of their competitors from the United States, Japan, and Europe in transferring to Mexico their more work-intensive operations. Mexican industry shows no signs of a real increase in scientific and technological content, despite all the enthusiastic news coverage of that country's economic boom. International firms engaged in globalization are rushing to Mexico, attracted by two types of rents: the rent brought by the proximity to the bottomless market of the United States and the rent afforded by a seemingly inexhaustible supply of workers subject to discipline and likely to accept salaries that are little more than half the basic salary in South Korea, and much less than half that of Taiwan. The first component of the recipe for liberalizing into development would seem to be resistance to that sort of "modernization" throughout Latin America.

A second, fundamental component of the recipe would be to create among all the social forces inside the Southern Cone a consensus that recognizes how important it is for the economies of the region to catch up with the incipient sociotechnological paradigm that will supersede Fordism. In the industrial age only industrialization ensures the creation of the material conditions, in terms of employment and gross national product, necessary for a country to acquire the degree of liberty in the disposition of its own destiny that characterizes effective modernization. To be modern in our time, a country must do more than simply adopt the garb of induced industrialization. What distinguishes a true late industrializer is the determination and the ability to arrive at the technological frontier of the time.

In sum, the main challenge confronting Brazil and its neighbors of the Southern Cone as the world approaches the third industrial revolution is to adjust their economies to the demands of the new paradigm. This adjustment must be conducted within the framework of MERCOSUR, which is a regional project capable of mobilizing ample sectors of these societies. At the center of the initiative must be the generation of knowledge—both internally, through education, the creation of technical capacity, and support for research and development, and externally, through the selective search for foreign technology to be constructively absorbed into the local market.

Only then will Brazil and its neighbors succeed in producing a well-timed, well-conceived, and well-informed opening of their economies to the international market. These countries must keep their eyes wide open to world changes but take care never to lose touch with their national realities. In this way they will still be able to liberalize into development.

Notes

[1] The classic discussion of the theory of long waves is provided by Joseph A. Schumpeter, *Business Cycles* (New York: McGraw-Hill, 1939). The most comprehensive exposition is found in Joshua S. Goldstein, *Long Cycles* (New Haven, Conn.: Yale University Press, 1988). Christopher Freeman edited two well-known collections of modern interpretations of the theory: *Long Waves in the World Economy* (London: Frances Pinter, 1984) and *Design, Innovation and Cycles* (London: F. Pinter, 1986). Also worth reading are J. J. van Duijn, *The Wave in Economic Life* (London: George Allen & Unwin, 1983) and Giovanni Dosi, *Technical Change and Industrial Transformation* (New York: Macmillan Press, 1984).

[2] An excellent introduction to the historical problem of "Fordism" is given by Annemieke J. M. Roobeek, "The Crisis in Fordism and a New Technological Paradigm," *Futures* 19, no. 2 (April 1987): 129–54.

[3] See Samuel Bowles, David M. Gordon, and Thomas E. Weisskopf, *Beyond the Waste Land* (New York: Anchor Books, 1984); David P. Calleo, *Beyond American Hegemony* (New York: Basic Books, 1987); Robert W. Cox, *Production, Power, and World Order* (New York: Columbia University Press, 1987); Robert Gilpin, *The Political Economy of International Relations* (Princeton, N. J.: Princeton University Press, 1987); Paul Kennedy, *The Rise and Fall of the Great Powers* (London: Unwin Hyman, 1988); Michael L. Dertouzos, Richard K. Lester, and Robert M. Solow, *Made in America* (New York: Harper Perennial, 1990); Joseph S. Nye, Jr., *Bound to Lead* (New York: Basic Books, 1990); James P. Womack, Daniel T. Jones, and Daniel Roos, *The Machine That Changed the World* (New York: Rawson Associates, 1990); and Henry R. Nau, *The Myth of America's Decline* (New York: Oxford University Press, 1990).

[4] Cf. Hanns W. Maull, "Germany and Japan: The New Civilian Powers," *Foreign Affairs* 69, no. 5 (Winter 1990/91): 91–106.

[5] Gérard Lafay and Colette Herzog, "La Création des Avantages Comparatifs dans les Activités de Haute Technologie," *Revue D'Economie Industrielle* 55 (Winter/Spring, 1991).

[6] An accessible publication on the paradigmatic competition is the magazine *Futures*, published in the United Kingdom by Butterworths. Examples of interesting articles on the subject are Pierre-Noel Giraud, "Japan at the Turning Point," 19, no. 4 (August 1987): 385–402; and Martin Kenney and Richard Florida, "Japan's Role in a Post-Fordist Age," 21, no. 2 (April 1989): 136–151.

[7] On the connection between energy and industrial change in Japan, see Daniel I. Okimoto, ed., *Japan's Economy* (Boulder, Colo.: Westview Press, 1982), chap. 2; also Yukio Kaneko, "Changes in Japan's Industrial Structure since the Oil Crisis" in *The Developing Economies* (Tokyo: Institute of Developing Economies) 18, no. 4 (Dec. 1980): 484–501.

[8] Cf. Thomas S. Kuhn, *The Structure of Scientific Revolutions* (Chicago: University of Chicago Press, 1976).

[9] Giovanni Dosi (see book cited in note 1) in particular has studied the problem of technological trajectories.

[10] Ichizo Yamauchi, "Long Range Strategic Planning in Japanese R&D," in Christopher Freeman, ed., *Design, Innovation and Long Cycles* (London: Frances Pinter, 1986).

[11] Kenney and Florida, "Japan's Role in a Post-Fordist Age," 137.

[12] Robert Gilpin, *The Political Economy of International Relations* (Princeton, N.J.: Princeton University Press, 1987).

[13] Gilpin, *Political Economy*, 75–76.

[14] Bela Balassa, *The Newly Industrializing Countries in the World Economy* (New York: Pergamon Press, 1981), primarily essay 1.

[15] There is a growing literature on the post–World War II experiences of Taiwan and South Korea. As suggestions for further reading I propose Lawrence S. Lau, *Models of Development* (San Francisco: Institute for Contemporary Studies, 1986); Shirley W. Y. Kuo, *The Taiwan Economy in Transition* (Boulder, Colo.: Westview Press, 1983); K. T. Li, *The Evolution of Policy behind Taiwan's Development Success* (New Haven, Conn.: Yale University Press, 1988); Alice H. Amsden, *Asia's Next Giant* (New York: Oxford University Press, 1989); and Byung Nak Song, *The Rise of the Korean Economy* (New York: Oxford University Press, 1990).

[16] For the story of JCRR, see Joseph A. Yager, *Transforming Agriculure in Taiwan* (Ithaca, N.Y.: Cornell University Press, 1988).

[17] Janne E. Nolan, *Military Industry in Taiwan and South Korea* (London: Macmillan, 1986).

[18] The reconstruction of American officials' participation in the political and economic organization of the mercantilist states of East Asia in the post–World War II era is a relatively new field of academic study. Alice H. Amsden, "The State and Taiwan's Economic Development," in Peter B. Evans, Dietrich Rueschemeyer, and Theda Skocpol, eds., *Bringing the State Back In* (Cambridge, U.K.: Cambridge University Press, 1985) is a pioneering work on that subject. One of the more recent and comprehensive studies is Tun-jen Cheng, "Political Regimes and Development Strategies: South Korea and Taiwan," in Gary Gereffi and Donald T. Wyman, *Manufacturing Miracles* (Princeton, N.J.: Princeton University Press, 1990).

[19] Bradford Colin, "Opciones para la Reactivación Latinoamericana en los Años Noventa," *Revista de la CEPAL* (United Nations Economic Commission for Latin America and the Caribbean, Santiago, Chile) no. 44 (August 1991): 109–16.

[20] Edward K. Y. Chen, "Trade Policy in Asia," in Seiji Naya, Miguel Urrutia, Shelley Mark, and Alfredo Fuentes, eds. *Lessons in Development* (San Francisco: International Center for Economic Growth, 1989).

[21] A far from exhaustive list of books on Japan's developmental state and its influence on East Asia would include Chalmers Johnson, *MITI and the Japanese Miracle* (Stanford, Cal.: Stanford University Press, 1982); Robert Wade, *Governing the Market* (Princeton, N.J.: Princeton University Press, 1991); Frederic C. Deyo, ed., *The Political Economy of the New Asian Industrialism* (Ithaca, N.Y.: Cornell University Press, 1987); Gordon White, ed., *Developmental States in East Asia* (London: Macmillan, 1988); Helen Hughes, *Achieving Industrialization in East Asia* (Cambridge, U.K.: Cambridge University Press, 1988); Garry Rodan, *The Political Economy of Singapore's Industrialization* (London: Macmillan, 1989); and Hadi Soesastro and Mari Pangestu, eds., *Technological Challenge in the Asia-Pacific Economy* (London: Allen & Unwin, 1990).

[22] The East Asian NICs' push toward the twenty-first century and complete industrialization should be followed mainly in periodicals, among which *The Far*

Eastern Economic Review is indispensable. But books with this perspective have appeared: Stephan Haggard and Chung-in Moon, eds., *Pacific Dynamics* (Boulder, Colo.: Westview Press, 1989); John P. Hardt and Young C. Kim, *Economic Cooperation in the Asia-Pacific Region* (Boulder, Colo.: Westview Press, 1989); and John P. Hardt and Young C. Kim, *Economic Cooperation in the Asia-Pacific Region* (Boulder, Colo.: Westview Press, 1990). Some excellent chapters can be found in Robert E. Evenson and Gustav Ranis, *Science and Technology: Lessons for Development Policy* (Boulder, Colo.: Westview Press, 1990).

23 Cf. Andrew J. Rotter, *The Path to Vietnam* (Ithaca, N.Y.: Cornell University Press, 1987), 23.

24 There is a vast amount of literature available in Brazil, in Portuguese, on the truncated development of Latin American economies. A classic work available in English is Celso Furtado, *Economic Development of Latin America* (Cambridge, U.K.: Cambridge University Press, 1970). A sample of books by British and American scholars includes Jordan M. Young, *The Brazilian Revolution of 1930 and the Aftermath* (New Brunswick, N.J.: Rutgers University Press, 1967); Robert T. Daland, *Brazilian Planning* (Chapel Hill, N.C.: University of North Carolina Press, 1967); Stanley J. Stein and Barbara H. Stein, *The Colonial Heritage of Latin America* (New York: Oxford University Press, 1970); Julio Cotler and Richard R. Fagen, *Latin America and the United States: The Changing Political Realities* (Stanford, Cal.: Stanford University Press, 1974); Richard R. Fagen, ed., *Capitalism and the State in U.S.-Latin American Relations* (Stanford, Cal.: Stanford University Press, 1979); and Miguel S. Wionczek, *Some Key Issues for the World Periphery* (Oxford, U.K.: Pergamon Press, 1982) is important for Mexico.

25 Cf. Abraham F. Lowenthal, "'Liberal', 'Radical,' and 'Bureaucratic' Perspectives on U.S. Latin American Policy: The Alliance for Progress in Retrospective," in Cotler and Fagen, *Latin America and the United States*, 214 (cited in note 24).

26 William H. Branson, "Trade and Structural Interdependence between the United States and the Newly Industrializing Countries," in Colin I. Bradford, Jr., and William H. Branson, eds., *Trade and Structural Change in Pacific Asia* (Chicago: University of Chicago Press, 1987), 28.

27 An excellent recent book on this theme is Fernando Fajnzylber, *Unavoidable Industrial Restructuring in Latin America* (Durham, S.C.: Duke University Press, 1990).

28 See Peter B. Evans, *Dependent Development: The Alliance of Multinational, State and Local Capital in Brazil* (Princeton, N.J.: Princeton University Press, 1979).

29 Werner Baer, *A Industrialização e o Desenvolvimento Econômico do Brasil* (Rio de Janeiro: Fundação Getlio Vargas, 1988), 337–60. This is the seventh edition of a widely read book in Brazil. Its successive editions include new work by Professor Baer, and it is difficult to locate the originally published English text.

30 Cf. Barbara Stallings, "The Role of Foreign Capital in Economic Development," in Gereffi and Wyman, *Manufacturing Miracles*, 56–89 (cited in note 18).

31 For a theoretical approach to the problem of late industrialization, the classic work is Friedrich List, *The National System of Political Economy*, translated from German into English in London in 1885 and reprinted by August M. Kelley Publishers (New York, 1966). Also recomended are A. Gerschenkron, *Economic Backwardness in Historical Perspective* (Cambridge, Mass.: Harvard

University Press, 1962); David S. Landes, *The Unbound Prometheus* (Cambridge, U.K.: Cambridge University Press, 1969); Angus Maddison, *Phases of Capitalist Development* (Oxford, U.K.: Oxford University Press, 1982); and Robert W. Cox, *Production, Power, and World Order* (New York: Columbia University Press, 1987).

32 Francisco R. Sagasti, "Crisis and Challenge: Science and Technology in the Future of Latin America," *Futures*, 21, no. 2 (April 1989): 161–68.

33 Colin Bradford, "Opciones para la Reactivación Latinoamericana en los Años Noventa" *Revista de la CEPAL* (United Nations Economic Commission for Latin America and the Caribbean, Santiago, Chile) no. 44 (August 1991): 109–16.

Chapter 4

The Efficiency of State Intervention in the Economy

Fernando de Holanda Barbosa

Events in the socialist bloc have quite clearly demonstrated the complete failure of countries that have adopted the system of central planning to achieve a sustained improvement in the welfare of their populations. The undeniable conclusion at the end of the century is that the market is society's most efficient mechanism of resource allocation. This does not mean, however, that the state should never intervene in economic affairs. Indeed, in all developed countries—in different ways and to different degrees—such intervention plays a vital role.

According to economic theory, state intervention is justified by market failures such as natural monopoly; the existence of public goods, externalities, or incomplete information; and the absence of certain markets. Whether or not some of these situations represent sufficient justification for state intervention is a matter of deep controversy among economists. This chapter does not analyze the debate that exists in economic literature on this issue. It simply assumes that for economic or political reasons the state does indeed intervene in market function, and then analyzes the efficiency of that intervention.

An analysis of the efficiency of state intervention in the economy must naturally involve an investigation of government failure, which the pertinent literature attributes to certain types of restraints (such as scant information or knowledge) and administrative-political limitations. This chapter examines the extent to which the institutional framework for state action causes intervention to fail by allowing those in charge to take arbitrary and casuistic decisions that increase market inefficiency. This analysis focuses on two areas of the Brazilian economy: (1) state-owned monopolies and (2) corporations of mixed ownership in which the state is a controlling shareholder.

The chapter is divided into four sections. The first section describes the mechanisms that regulate the prices of electricity, telecommunications services, and refined oil products. The second section analyzes the actual performance record of the regulated prices of these goods and services during the 1970-1990 period. The third section develops a simple theoretical scheme to analyze the manner in which the stock market can help to enhance the efficiency of state-owned corporations with private shareholders. And, finally, the fourth section offers some conclusions and suggestions for the future.

Price Regulation in Oil Products, Electricity, and Telecommunications

In the past thirty years, the Brazilian government has regulated the prices of electricity, telecommunications services, and oil products. Responsibility for the regulation of each price has rested with branches of the executive power that became departments of the Ministry of Infrastructure when the Collor government introduced an administrative reform. The government's pricing policy over this period reveals four basic characteristics:

1. Price regulation is based on the principle of the rate of return of capital;
2. The price for each product or service is kept artificially uniform throughout the country;
3. The regulating agencies use a complex and varied system of cross subsidies, not only because of the maintenance of uniform prices but also because of different objectives of economic policy; and
4. There has been no concern for criteria of economic efficiency.

The Prices of Oil Products

The agency initially responsible for determining the price of oil products was the National Petroleum Council (CNP). It was succeeded by the National Department of Fuels (DNC) of the Ministry of Infrastructure under an administrative reform introduced by the Collor government.

The formula used by the CNP to calculate the prices of oil products was changed on several occasions. From 1954 to 1964 the ex-refinery price of each product was obtained by adding the single tax and the port and customs expenses to the price of the imported product. The selling price to the consumer was the same as the ex-refinery price plus the gross profit margin from distribution and resale. The cost of transport to cities in the interior of the country was added to the selling price to the consumer.

This criterion was changed in 1964 when the CNP began to stipulate periodically the ex-refinery unit price (excluding the single tax that is part of it) of the oil products listed and produced in the country by multiplying the coefficients enumerated in Table 4.1 by the average CIF (charge-in-freight) cost (in the national currency and by unit of volume) of the crude oil imported in the previous trimester. The CNP was authorized in 1964 to raise the coefficients in Table 4.1 in order to adjust the ex-refinery prices to the financial needs of the Petrobrás investment program.

Several other elements were added to the ex-refinery price. Denominated "items," they were actually disguised taxes included in an invoicing price. (Taxes had to be disguised because it was technically illegal to implement a tax without congressional approval.) The selling price to the consumer was the sum of the invoicing price and the margin for distribution and resale.

In 1966 the criterion changed again. The main justifications for this change were as follows:

1. A preference for basing the price of oil products on production costs, the structure of the national market, and international trade relations;
2. The need to guarantee profitability for the national refining section; and
3. The need to make the fiscal protection of oil products explicit so as to monitor more accurately the real results of the refining operations.

TABLE 4.1
THE PRICE OF OIL PRODUCTS:
LAW 4452 OF MAY 11, 1964

Product	Multiplying coefficients of the CIF cost of crude oil
Liquid gas	2.30
Aviation gasoline	2.15
Type A gasoline	2.20
Type B gasoline	2.60
Aviation kerosene	1.80
Kerosene	2.30
Diesel oil	2.25
Fuel oil	1.70
Lubricant oils	5.50 to 7.00

SOURCE: Brazilian Law 4452, passed May 11, 1964.

The average price of oil from the refinery was thereafter calculated by the sum of the following unit costs, gathered into four groups:

- Group I—Costs affected by the international market prices for crude oil and other imported consumer materials, and by the exchange rate;
- Group II—Labor costs;
- Group III—Other variable costs depending on the internal situation of prices within the country; and
- Group IV—Depreciation, amortization, and return of invested capital.

The average price of oil from the refinery calculated by the sum of these four costs defined the price of type A gasoline; the other prices were calculated by applying the coefficients in Table 4.2, which set up the structure of relative prices, excluding taxes from oil products.

In 1977 another change occurred, establishing the mechanism that has prevailed until now. The formula for calculating the unit price of the refinery oil was not altered; instead, the refinery unit price was no longer used to define the price of gasoline, and thence the prices of the other oil products, but rather to define the unit revenue for Petrobrás on the sale of any product.

As the production process in the oil industry is a joint process, it would have been too difficult to compute the cost of

TABLE 4.2
THE PRICE OF OIL PRODUCTS: DECREE LAW NO. 61

Product	Multiplying coefficients of the ex-refinery price of type A gasoline
Liquid gas	1.05
Type B gasoline	1.18
Kerosene	1.35
Diesel oil	1.00
Fuel oil	0.72

SOURCE: Brazilian Decree Law No. 61.

each product individually, so the new method sets the price of an "average" product, which is calculated to cover the four groups of costs. The Petrobrás unit revenue on the sale of any product is the same as the unit cost of the average product, and this revenue is called the average refinery value. In symbols, we have

$$C = C_{\mathrm{I}} + C_{\mathrm{II}} + C_{\mathrm{III}} + C_{\mathrm{IV}}$$

where $C_{\mathrm{I}}, C_{\mathrm{II}}, C_{\mathrm{III}}$, and C_{IV} are the unit costs of each group, and C is the total unit cost, or the average refinery value. (The average refinery value is the *sum* of the four Cs; it is also total unit cost.)

The prices for the various refined oil products, $P_i, i = 1, \ldots, n$, are obtained from the following conditions:

$$\sum_{i=1}^{n} P_i q_j = C \sum_{i=1}^{n} q_i$$

where q_i is the volume of the ith oil product sold on the domestic market. This formula allows the prices of the products to be altered without changing the average refinery value. For instance, if the price of gasoline is raised and that of liquid gas is lowered, average refinery value will not change. In fact, the prices of the products can be established in such a way that the weighted average is the same as the average refinery value. That is,

$$\sum_{i=1}^{n} w_i r_i = C$$

where the w_i weights are given by

$$w_i = \frac{q_i}{\sum_{j=1}^{n} q_j} \qquad i = 1, \ldots, n$$

This formula thus permits a system of cross subsidies by which the consumer of one product subsidizes the consumer of another without affecting the profitability of Petrobrás. The oil products included in the calculation of the average refinery value account for 95 percent of the refineries' total production volume. From the price of the refinery one reaches the invoicing price, then the distributor's invoicing price, and finally the consumer's price, adding the various components. The invoicing of the refinery and distributor includes a portion corresponding to the Prices Uniformization Fund (FUP), which is administered by the DNC, in order to render feasible another system of cross subsidies by which the prices of oil products are made uniform throughout Brazil.

ELECTRICITY RATES

Brazil's electricity tariff system is defined by the National Department of Water and Electricity (DNAEE), a branch of the Ministry of Infrastructure. This department establishes the producers' supply rates for the companies that distribute electric power, as well as the distributors' supply rates for the final consumer.

The rates are calculated according to the principle of service by cost, which was adopted when the Water Code was created in 1934. The purpose of this legal charter was to create a tariff that would express the costs of the system and be equitable to consumers, assigning to each group an equal fraction of the cost of the service rendered.

The Water Code stipulated that service by cost would comprise (1) all the expenses involved in operations, taxes, and rates of any nature incurred by the company; (2) reserves for depreciation; and (3) the company's capital return. The code also established that the evaluation of the capital actually used by the company, minus depreciation, should be calculated at historic cost rather than replacement cost and did not allow the nominal value to be corrected according to inflation. This anomalous situation was changed only about thirty years later, in 1964, when a monetary correction of tangible assets was allowed to be factored into the calculation of the value of the rate base, thereby protecting investments in the electricity sector from inflationary erosion.

The calculation of service by cost includes a component that corresponds to the return on capital invested in the electric power companies; the legal return on capital to be computed may be 10-12 percent at the discretion of the appropriate government authority. The following components of the total investment are considered in calculating the tariff:

1. The property and facilities actually in operation or use during the service;
2. Storeroom materials that are indispensable to the function or expansion of the company's electric system and administration; and
3. The working capital necessary for the company's transactions.

The value of the rate base is equal to the difference between the total investment and the sum of the following deductions:

1. Reserve for depreciation;
2. Reserve for amortization, if any;
3. Advance payments, contributions, and donations to the property and facilities included in the total investments;
4. The value of the setup costs of the property and facilities for future use, and of union property for use in special cases; and
5. The balance of the outstanding results account.

The difference between the return from the investment of the percentage approved by the conceding authority and the return verified at the end of the fiscal period is registered in the concessionaire's outstanding results account so that any excessive or insufficient return can be set right.

Also computed in the service cost is an annual quota of 5 percent on the total investment, deposited in twelfths in two Electrobrás accounts. The General Reversion Account for Clearing of Returns (RENCOR) is moved by Electrobrás in cases of reversion, expropriation of public utility electricity, or loans to concessionaires for the purpose of expanding services. The General Guarantee Reserve Account provides resources to guarantee the economic and financial equilibrium of the concessions and is moved by Eletrobrás on express instructions from the DNAEE. The legal return on capital to the concessionaires participating in the plans for investment of the General Guarantee Reserve resources can be up to 10 percent a year, at the discretion of the former Ministry of Mines and Energy.

The supply of electric power increases in cost through the generation-transmission-distribution chain. As the tension level of the supply of electric power decreases, more equipment is added and new operational and maintenance structures become necessary. For tariff purposes consumers are classified into two large groups: (1) group A, high tension, and (2) group B, low tension. The latter group includes consumers of energy up to a tension of 2.3 kilovolts (kv); they are divided into four subgroups: (1) group B1, residential; (2) group B2, rural; (3) group B3, commercial; and (4) group B4, public lighting.

The tariff system applied to group B1 (residential) is divided into consumer levels so as to give those who use fewer kilowatt hours lower energy costs and to provide a scheme of cross subsidies between the various classes of consumers. Table 4.3 shows the discounts conceded to residential consumers of electric power at different periods.

Two types of tariffs are applied to group B2 (rural), one for the rural property itself and another, lower tariff for rural cooperatives. Group B3, embracing general commerce and small industries, is subject to a single tariff. Group B4 (public

TABLE 4.3
DISCOUNTS IN ELECTRICITY RATES FOR RESIDENTIAL CONSUMERS

Consumption Interval (kwh)	Month/Year					
	April 1990	December 1989	October 1989	March 1985	May 1980	February 1979
0–30	70%	70%	89%	68%	35%	0%
31–100	52	52	72	37	0	0
101–200	40	40	65	37	0	0
201–300	8	8	16	16	0	0
301–500	0	0	0	16	0	0
Over 500	0	0	0	0	0	0

SOURCE: Eletrobrás.

lighting) is largely made up of city councils responsible for municipal lighting; here, too, a single tariff is enforced.

The electricity rates applied to group B are monomial: that is, consumers are charged only for the consumption of electric power. Group A is subject to two tariff systems, the conventional and the horoseasonal. The tariff in the conventional system is binomial, with one component for potency (kw) and the other for energy consumption (kwh). The horoseasonal system divides the day into peak and off-peak periods and the year into dry and wet seasons. Invoicing is based on peak and off-peak consumption for each period of the year. Demand is invoiced at peak and off-peak consumption for each period of the year, whether the season is dry or wet. In both tariff systems group A consumers are classified at various levels of tension.

Electricity rates were equalized for the whole country in 1974, thus giving rise to another system of cross subsidies by dissociating the tariff from the service cost. The practice of equalization led to changes in the methodology the DNAEE used to calculate the tariffs. Because the tariff level for each electric power company was determined by tension level, which reflected its costs, the DNAEE decided that there was no need for each company to calculate its costs, only to ensure that the revenue from the tariffs covered its overall costs for the electrical sector.

Companies began to cease presenting their schedule of costs by tension level, but rather presented their overall costs. With the use of this data the DNAEE gradually equalized the companies' tariffs (so as to equalize prices without respect to each company's costs) but nevertheless continued to classify consumers by tension level. As a result, the tariffs based on tension level inevitably became distanced from the principle of service by cost for each consumer group.

For tariff equalization to be compatible with the companies' costs, the supply rates between companies had to be differentiated, because the price charged the final consumer within each consumer group became the same by law. To prevent many companies from having a real return over capital invested that was either greater or less than the legally stipulated limits, the following mechanism was adopted: for those companies with a return above the legal limit, the cost of the bought energy is raised by increasing the supply tariff, while for those companies whose return falls below the legal limit, the supply tariff is lowered. Thus, in order to guarantee the economic and financial equilibrium of the concessionaire companies as demanded by law, the supply tariff has become the adjustment element in the distribution of financial resources. When this procedure is inadequate to ensure a company's profitability, the General Guarantee Reserve Account is used; instead of being a percentage of the value of the facilities, the amount contributed by each company is determined by the positive difference between the company's return and the average return of the electricity sector. This arrangement has allowed a greater volume of resources to be transferred through the General Guarantee Reserve by removing the supply tariffs as an adjustment variable for the financial resources of the electricity sector.

The equalization of rates has caused revenue to be transferred from regions where companies produce electric power more efficiently at lower costs to companies with higher costs. Given the generalized dissatisfaction of the concessionaire companies jeopardized by the mechanism of resource transfers, the DNAEE replaced the General Guarantee Reserve Account with the RENCOR, limiting the return to 12 percent and guaranteeing a minimum return of 10 percent through credits on the RENCOR account. When the rate of return lies between 10 percent and 12 percent, the concessionaire company pays neither the RENCOR nor the reversion quota and receives no resources from the RENCOR. Conversely, when the rate of return is below 10 percent, the concessionaire company receives credit from the RENCOR account for an amount equal to the difference between the value that it should have according to the legal rate and the value actually realized in the company's operation.

The Telecommunications Services Tariff

Specific legislation in the telecommunications sector began, for all practical purposes, with the National Telecommunications Code created in 1962. This code granted powers to the National Council on Telecommunications (CONTEL) to determine the criteria for fixing and readjusting tariffs for telecommunications services; the council was subordinated to the Ministry of Communications when that body was created in 1967. CONTEL determined that tariffs would be stipulated in the form of service by cost, which would include exploration expenses, taxes, and fair return on investment.

Exploration expenses were defined as those relating to the conservation, operation, and administration of the property and facilities and applied to the services rendered, such as expenses involving personnel, materials and services, and provisions for depreciation and the amortization of intangible assets. The expenses relating to amortization and interest payments in national and foreign currency must be covered, respectively, by the depreciation component and the return on investment, which was fixed at 12 percent of the value of the capital invested.

Users of telecommunications services pay the same tariff anywhere in the country for a given service. This principle began with the creation of Telebrás, when a nationwide standardization was established for the quality of the services rendered. The idea behind this pricing policy was that the same services should have similar tariffs regardless of their production costs.

Since the cost curves of its various companies are different, Telebrás was set up to redistribute revenue from interurban and international telephone service, through which less profitable companies receive a greater percentage of the tariff.

The transfer of revenue from interurban and international telephone service was justified on the principle that all such calls begin at a local station belonging to a certain operating company, which therefore incurs costs in making the connection. The concessionaire for interurban and international telephone services, Embratel, transfers part of the revenue obtained from each call to the local operating company where the connection originated. The percentage transferred varies from one company to the other, according to the profitability of the company in the preceding fiscal period. This practice of dividing the revenue stimulates inefficiency, since the companies with the worst results receive heftier transfers of resources.

Pricing Regulation: The Performance Record

This section presents an analysis of the performance record of regulated prices for refined oil products, electricity, and telecommunications services during the last twenty years. It shows that the institutional regulatory framework did not work in practice, but rather brought about rates of return on capital that were different from, and even below, the regulated rates.

OIL PRODUCTS

Over the last twenty years, the world economy has been subjected to two adverse shocks and one favorable shock in the price of oil. The first shock occurred in 1973, quadrupling the average price of a barrel of imported oil in Brazil by 1974. The second shock, in 1979, saw the average price of the barrel jump 72 percent by 1980. The third shock happened in 1986, when the nominal price of a barrel of oil fell 50 percent against the average price in 1985.

TABLE 4.4
REAL PRICES OF OIL-REFINED PRODUCTS: 1970–1990 (1970 = 100)

Year	Gasoline	Kerosene	Diesel	Fuel oil	Liquid petroleum gas (LPG)
1970	100.0	100.0	100.0	100.0	NA
1971	102.7	103.3	102.6	103.8	NA
1972	109.3	114.7	111.5	115.0	NA
1973	110.3	112.8	109.1	111.3	100.0
1974	165.0	129.3	116.5	125.0	121.6
1975	202.4	NA	129.7	133.8	128.4
1976	237.9	133.2	136.8	147.5	126.2
1977	220.0	141.3	155.0	153.8	119.6
1978	226.2	141.0	149.4	148.8	113.3
1979	229.1	154.6	162.9	180.0	100.2
1980	324.2	189.9	173.5	305.0	77.5
1981	325.7	179.6	198.2	430.0	75.0
1982	289.5	192.1	205.0	392.5	70.4
1983	272.9	195.4	192.9	425.0	77.9
1984	246.9	194.8	204.7	433.8	81.6
1985	224.9	180.4	188.8	402.5	73.7
1986	204.2	134.8	136.8	295.0	50.9
1987	264.8	116.3	122.4	285.0	52.7
1988	202.7	100.0	116.2	236.3	42.1
1989	153.5	94.6	92.9	182.5	32.0
1990	162.3	103.0	95.6	203.8	39.5

SOURCE: Petrobrás.

Table 4.4 shows what happened to the real prices of the main oil products in the period between 1970 and 1990. The real price of gasoline rose slightly between 1970 and 1973. In 1974, after the first oil crisis, the average real price of gasoline rose 50 percent from its price in 1973 and went on rising until 1976, when its price was more than double the average price of 1973. From 1977 to 1979 the average real price remained slightly below the average price of 1976, while after the second crisis, from 1979–1980, it grew 42 percent. In 1981 the real price of gasoline reached its peak, becoming almost three times more expensive than in 1973. From 1981 onward the real price of gasoline began to drop, and in 1987 the price was equal to 63 percent of the average price of 1981. There was an increase in 1987 of 30 percent against the average price of the previous year, and in 1989–1990, the real price of gasoline fell below the average price of 1974, 47 percent more than the 1973 price.

The average annual price of kerosene rose by 15 percent between 1970 and 1973, and in 1974 it again increased 15 percent against the average price of 1973. During the rest of the 1970s the real price of kerosene rose slightly, and in 1980 the average price grew 23 percent from its 1979 level. From 1980 to 1984 the price of kerosene remained at practically the same level, and from then it declined until 1990. From 1988 to 1990 the average real price of kerosene was lower than the average price in effect in 1973 before the first oil crisis.

In the early 1970s the real price of diesel presented no great fluctuations, showing a moderate growth of 9 percent in 1973 from its average price in 1970. One year after the first oil shock the real average price of diesel oil had risen only 15 percent, revealing the then-current strategy of not internally transferring the rise in the price of imported oil. The strategy of gradually increasing the price of diesel from 1974 to 1979 caused the 1979 price to reach 47 percent above the average 1973 price. In 1980, after the second oil crisis, the price of diesel rose only 6 percent from its average price in 1979, and in 1981 the price was raised 14 percent. In 1982 another 3 percent increase occurred in relation to the average price of the year before, when the average real price of diesel reached its peak for 1970–1980. After 1984 the real price of diesel began to fall, only to show a slight recovery in 1990. In 1988 and 1990 the real price of diesel was lower than the prices in effect in the early 1970s before the first oil shock.

From 1970 to 1973 the price of fuel oil followed the same pattern as the prices of the other oil products, the real price in 1973 being around 11 percent higher than the average price in 1970. In the year after the first oil shock the price of fuel oil rose 12 percent. With the strategy of gradually increasing prices in the following years, the price of fuel oil went up: in 1979 it was 62 percent higher than in 1973. After the second oil shock, in 1979, the price kept going up, increasing 69 percent in 1980 and 41 percent in 1981. Between 1981 and 1984 the average real price of fuel oil remained at a reasonably steady level and then began a decreasing trajectory that was interrupted in 1990. Unlike the price of diesel and kerosene but similar to that of gasoline, the real price of fuel oil in 1989 and 1990 was higher than the real prices in effect not only in the early 1970s but throughout that decade.

In the year following the first oil shock the price of liquid petroleum gas (LPG) increased 22 percent, and in 1975 it continued to go up until it reached its peak for the period under analysis. From 1976 to 1982 the price of LPG dropped, its value in 1982 amounting to only 70 percent of the average price in effect before the first crisis, despite the rise in the price of imported oil with the second oil shock. Between 1983 and 1985 the price of LPG stayed relatively steady. In 1986 the Cruzado plan was implemented. This was a heterodox economic stabilization program, which included a wage-price freeze and the creation of a new currency (the cruzado) and which was aimed primarily at halting high inflation. With the advent of the Cruzado plan, the price of LPG dropped, only to recover somewhat in 1987 and then fall again, to reach its lowest value ever in 1989, when it equaled 32 percent of the average price of 1983.

The Brazilian strategy of adjusting the prices of refined products in response to each oil shock involved changing the structure of relative prices, with the weight of the adjustment falling on gasoline and fuel oil. Table 4.5 shows the evolution of relative prices in the 1970–1990 period, taking the price of diesel as the unit. Notice that the price of kerosene was reasonably steady in relation to that of diesel throughout the period. This was not true of the price of fuel oil, which after the 1980s practically doubled against the relative price it had maintained during the 1970s.

The relative price of gasoline, which was about 20 percent higher than that of diesel from 1970 to 1973, increased somewhat

TABLE 4.5
THE PRICES OF REFINED PRODUCTS
RELATIVE TO THE PRICE OF DIESEL: 1970–1990

Year	Gasoline	Kerosene	Fuel oil	Liquid petroleum gas (LPG)
1970	1.20	1.00	0.24	NA
1971	1.20	1.09	0.24	NA
1972	1.18	1.11	0.24	NA
1973	1.22	1.12	0.24	3.67
1974	1.70	1.20	0.25	4.18
1975	1.88	0.24	3.97	NA
1976	2.09	1.05	0.24	3.70
1977	1.88	0.99	0.23	3.09
1978	1.82	1.02	0.23	3.04
1979	1.69	1.03	0.26	2.46
1980	2.25	1.18	0.41	1.79
1981	1.98	0.98	0.51	1.52
1982	1.70	1.01	0.45	1.38
1983	1.70	1.10	0.52	1.62
1984	1.45	1.03	0.50	1.60
1985	1.43	1.03	0.50	1.56
1986	1.80	1.06	0.51	1.49
1987	2.60	1.03	0.55	1.73
1988	2.10	0.93	0.48	1.45
1989	1.99	1.10	0.46	1.38
1990	2.04	1.17	0.50	1.66

SOURCE: Petrobrás.

in 1974 but did not follow as regular a pattern as fuel oil during the rest of the period. Unlike fuel oil, gasoline did not double in price except in 1987, when its relative price was the highest of the entire 1970–1990 period.

Despite occasional erratic fluctuations, the price of liquid petroleum gas showed a declining trend from 1973 to 1990 relative to the price of diesel. Between 1980 and 1990 its average price was 45 percent of the average price it maintained from 1973 to 1979.

We can conclude from this analysis of the structure of relative prices and the mechanism of fixing the prices of oil products that after the first oil shock a system of cross subsidies was used, in which gasoline and fuel oil subsidized diesel and LPG.

ELECTRICITY

Table 4.6, which records the average annual electricity rates from 1970 to 1990, shows the evolution of the real price of electricity for residential, commercial, and industrial customers using 13.8 kv tension and for industrial consumers using 138 kv tension. The real price was obtained by dividing the price in national currency by the general price index (IGP–DI) of the Getulio Vargas Foundation, and then dividing by the average exchange rate for the U.S. dollar in the month of June 1991. The consumption of electric power was measured by megawatt hour; the prices in Table 4.6 are thus expressed in dollars per megawatt hour.

TABLE 4.6
AVERAGE ANNUAL ELECTRICITY RATES, 1970–1990 (DOLLARS PER MEGAWATT HOUR)

	Users			
Year	Households	Commercial	Industrial low tension (13.8 kv)	Industrial high tension (138 kv)
1970	116.60	123.16	56.84	29.90
1971	121.32	128.14	57.32	27.13
1972	132.16	139.61	61.41	27.98
1973	128.64	135.89	59.77	27.24
1974	122.46	129.37	56.90	25.93
1975	134.43	141.80	64.49	31.88
1976	129.44	137.19	63.74	30.75
1977	120.45	129.26	63.46	30.11
1978	110.16	119.69	65.65	30.78
1979	112.04	118.18	61.21	29.79
1980	92.60	116.95	61.04	30.33
1981	84.97	119.48	68.94	35.62
1982	79.03	118.63	66.93	36.87
1983	70.32	105.56	58.76	33.61
1984	65.46	100.54	56.60	32.40
1985	58.27	98.35	59.11	33.01
1986	54.63	99.44	67.97	33.16
1987	63.35	111.52	66.36	38.51
1988	56.72	107.73	68.10	33.94
1989	42.55	85.25	54.37	26.68
1990	54.42	81.43	52.09	25.59

SOURCE: Eletrobrás.

The prices are measured on a cash basis, which means that the date of payment was taken into account. In a country with a traditonally high rate of inflation, prices differ depending on whether they are calculated on a cash or accrual basis because of the effect of inflation during the period from the measurement of electricity consumed to the moment the bill is paid.

From 1970 to 1979 the real price of residential electric power presented a slight variation of 13 percent, from $110.16 per megawatt hour in 1978 to $134.43 per megawatt hour in 1975, with an average value of $122.77 per megawatt hour. Between 1980 and 1986 the price fell from $92.60 to $54.63 and recovered slightly in 1987 when the average real price was $63.35, only to drop shortly thereafter. In 1988 and 1989 the real price of electricity for residential consumers was a little under half the prices of the 1970s.

The real prices of electricity for commercial consumers during the 1980s were lower than those of the previous decade. The highest cost was registered in 1975, at $141.80 per megawatt hour. The lowest prices for the period were registered in 1989 at $85.25 and in 1990 at $81.43.

The real price of electricity for industrial consumers supplied at a tension level of 13.8 kv remained reasonably stable from 1970 to 1980. The lowest price was registered in 1990 at $52.09 and the highest in 1981 at $68.94. The average value in these twenty-one years was $61.48. The real price reached its lowest levels in the last two years of the period.

The pattern of behavior of the real price of electrical energy for industrial consumers supplied at a tension level of 138 kv is similar to that of the real price for industrial consumers supplied at 13.8 kv. The real price underwent no great oscillations. The lowest price was $25.59 in 1990 and the highest was $38.51 in 1987. The real average price during the period was $31.01.

TELECOMMUNICATIONS

Table 4.7 clearly demonstrates the effects of the tariff policy in the telecommunications sector from 1976 to 1989, as illustrated by the telephone rates between the cities of Rio de Janeiro and São Paulo, evaluated relative to 1976 prices (the nominal value of the tariff was divided by the general price index of the Getulio Vargas Foundation). Until the middle of 1979 the real tariff remained reasonably steady and then began a process of gradual deterioration throughout the next decade. The average tariff in 1980 was already 75 percent of the previous year's average.

The situation worsened with the advent of the New Republic (the return to civilian government in 1985 after twenty-one years of military rule); the 1985 average was 39 percent of the 1979 value. In 1986 (the year of the Cruzado plan) the average rates dropped to 30 percent of their 1979 value. The real tariff remained quite low in 1987, 1988, and 1989, and improved only slightly in 1989 after varying tariff levels depending on the time of day were introduced by the Sarney government in September of 1988.

One possible reason for lowering the tariffs would have been to reduce costs, thus passing along a decreased service price to the consumer. However, as Table 4.7 shows, while the tariff fell from an index of 100 in 1976 to 28 in 1988, the cost index between these two years went from 100 to 88. Clearly, then, the cost reduction was not the reason tariffs were lowered. Tariffs fell because they were being used, contrary to declared principles, in a discretionary fashion to reduce inflation.

TABLE 4.7
TELECOMMUNICATIONS RATES AND COSTS: 1976–1989

Year	Rates	Costs
1976	100	100
1977	113	95
1978	112	90
1979	107	95
1980	81	93
1981	75	94
1982	69	95
1983	59	88
1984	51	81
1985	43	80
1986	31	74
1987	36	94
1988	28	88
1989	25	136

SOURCE: Telebrás.

Rates of Return on Capital

The performance record for the rates of return on capital for the oil, electricity, and telecommunications sectors did not diverge from that of the prices. Table 4.8 shows the rates of return on capital in these three sectors from 1973 to 1990. These rates tend to vary widely. The difference between the highest and the lowest rates for the rate of return on capital for Petrobrás was 21.2 percent, for Eletrobrás 7.7 percent, and for Telebrás 12 percent. They also tend, on the average, to fall below the regulated rate for their sector. The regulated rate for the telecommunications sector is 12 percent, but only in 1973 did the rate of return exceed this percentage. In the other years the rate remained well below 10 percent. The regulated rate for electricity is 10 percent, but the rate of return was greater than this in only two years (1974 and 1976) and below 10 percent in the other years. Petrobrás showed a larger variation but presented a higher average rate of return on capital than the other two sectors.

Table 4.8
Rates of Return on Capital: 1973–1990

Year	Oil (Petrobrás)	Electricity (Eletrobrás)	Telecommunications (Telebrás)
1973	15.6%	NA	13.0%
1974	17.3	10.4%	4.1
1975	18.7	NA	8.5
1976	23.1	11.4	8.3
1977	18.8	NA	11.2
1978	17.4	8.6	7.2
1979	11.2	NA	6.6
1980	12.7	7.7	8.8
1981	11.5	9.1	8.8
1982	8.0	6.7	7.7
1983	7.4	4.4	6.7
1984	7.7	5.8	6.6
1985	18.9	5.1	5.0
1986	22.9	3.7	3.6
1987	1.7	4.9	3.5
1988	6.5	5.8	5.6
1989	1.9	4.8	1.0
1990	9.5	NA	NA

Sources: Petrobrás, Eletrobrás, and Telebrás.

The Control and Management of Brazilian Corporations of Mixed Ownership

Thus far, economic analysis has failed to provide a theory that would allow society, in seeking to maximize social welfare, to choose between the creation of a private and a state-owned company. This choice is generally made on political rather than economic grounds. Yet it is important from an economist's standpoint to determine whether the form of private or state ownership has any bearing on the company's behavior.

In their classic work, Berle and Means[1] drew attention to the dissociation between the ownership and management of modern corporations. The objective of the administrators of such companies, they noted, is not to maximize the company's profits. In modern literature this is seen as a typical principal-agent problem, with the principal being the shareholder and the agent being the manager. Whereas the shareholder's aim is to maximize profits, the manager may have other objectives. The pertinent question is whether there are market mechanisms that can lead the manager to behave like a shareholder. This section investigates this problem in relation to Brazil's state-owned corporations, using a simple theoretical framework based on Williamson's 1964 model.[2]

Before beginning the analysis, we should note that Brazil's state-owned companies fall into two categories: public companies and corporations of mixed ownership. Both are private-law entities—public companies that adhere to private-sector laws and regulations. The public company is a corporate private-law entity, with the government's own and exclusive equity and capital, legally created to engage in economic activities. Companies of mixed ownership are corporate private-law entities legally created to engage in economic activities. They take the form of joint-stock companies whose shares, with voting rights, belong mostly to the government. These companies are not subject to bankruptcy, but their assets may be pledged and executed and the controlling corporation is subsidiarily responsible for its obligations. This chapter will deal only with the state-owned companies of mixed ownership—more specifically with those whose shares are traded on the stock market, such as Petrobrás, Eletrobrás, Telebrás, and other government-controlled enterprises.

Suppose that the aim of the manager (agent) is to maximize a utility function. One of the manager's goals is profit, although other variables may also receive consideration; for instance, the manager may be willing to trade off part of the profits for prestige, status, and power. Suppose that these variables can be represented by the company's output level (q). So the agent's objective is to maximize the utility function.

$$u = u(\pi, q), \quad \frac{\partial u}{\partial \pi} > 0, \quad \frac{\partial u}{\partial q} > 0$$

where π is the company's profits. Suppose also that the marginal utilities are positive and that the utility function is quasi-concave. Figure 4.1 shows indifference curves associated with this utility function. The managers do not have free choice because they are constrained not only by technology but also by the need to show profits that will satisfy the shareholders.

In Figure 4.1 curve *OCPEA* represents the company's profits as a function of the output level. At point *C* profits are at a maximum, the quantity produced equals q^*, and the company is efficient, since production costs are minimized.

When the company maximizes the utility function without having to satisfy a profit constraint, or if the existing profit constraint is not effective, point *E* of the tangency between the

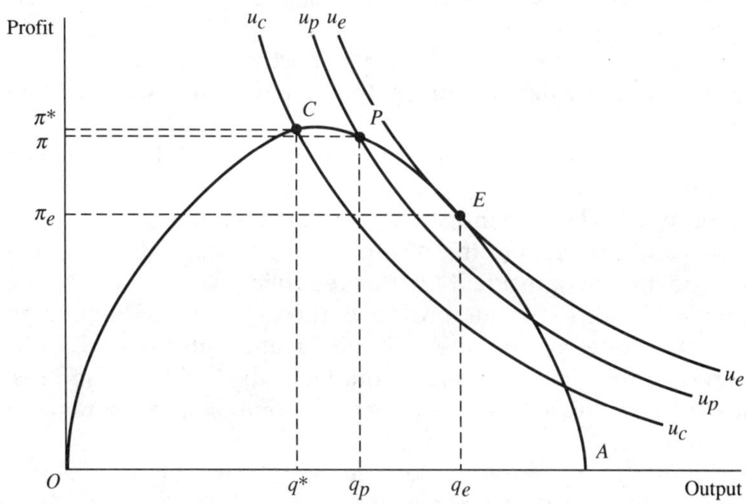

FIGURE 4.1 Corporation Behavior and Capital Ownership.

two curves is the optimal solution of the model. Imagine now that the shareholders wish for a profit level of π. In this case the solution of the model will be given by the intersection of the utility curve with the profit curve at point *P* of Figure 4.1.

In a company with private ownership of capital the shareholders have an incentive to discover the maximum profit that the company can achieve. When the shares are traded on the stock market, some people may be willing to assume control of the company if they detect unexplored profitable possibilities. If the information costs to actual and potential shareholders are negligible, the profit constraint should be near the value of the maximum profit, and the company equilibrium should be near point *C*, where profits are maximized and production costs minimized.

In a company of mixed ownership, in which the state holds control of the stock and the minority shareholders are unable to interfere in the management, the managers are not submitted to pressure from the stock market to factor into their decisions the profit level desired by the private shareholders. In such circumstances the company would operate at point *E* of Figure 4.1, since the managers would maximize the utility function without considering the profit constraint, and the share value would reflect this fact with a lower price than the profit constraint would require. Assuming that the managers of private companies and companies of mixed ownership share the same objectives, the behavior of their respective companies may be quite different, depending on the extent of the shareholder's influence.

The government holds majority stock control in Brazilian companies of mixed ownership, and the minority shareholders have practically no influence on administration. The presidents and directors of these companies are political appointees named by the president of the republic. As a result of the political nature of the positions there tends to be a high turnover rate among the presidents and directors of these corporations. Table 4.9 shows the length in office of the presidents and directors of two such corporations, Petrobrás and Eletrobrás.

From the inauguration of the first board of directors in May of 1954 until October of 1990 Petrobrás had twenty-three presidents and fifty directors. Eleven presidents and fifteen

TABLE 4.9
THE TENURE PERIOD FOR DIRECTORS OF
BRAZILIAN CORPORATIONS OF MIXED OWNERSHIP

Tenure period (years)	Petrobrás (1954–Oct. 1990)		Eletrobrás (1960–June 1990)	
	President	Directors	President	Directors
0–1	11	15	2	6
1–2	5	4	1	2
2–3	4	9	2	3
3–4	1	7	1	4
4–5	1	4	1	3
5–6	1	5	1	1
6–7	0	1	0	3
7–8	0	2	0	2
8–9	0	1	1	1
9–10	0	0	0	0
10–11	0	1	0	1
11–12	0	0	0	0
12–13	0	0	0	0
13–14	0	1	0	0
14–15	0	0	0	0
15–16	0	0	0	1
Total	23	50	9	27

SOURCES: Petrobrás and Eletrobrás.

directors occupied their positions for less than one year, while only three presidents remained for over three years. More stability is observed among the directors, with twenty-three (of a total of fifty) remaining in office for over three years.

The turnover of the board of directors of Eletrobrás was much smaller than that of Petrobrás during this period. In both cases, however, turnover increased in the last ten years. These facts show that the present mechanism for selecting directors deserves reconsideration. Surely the economic performance of these companies is not immune to such frequent changes in administrative ranks.

It is also important to note that the remuneration of these directors does not depend on economic performance, and no mechanism is presently in place to stimulate efficiency and profitability.

The manner in which the stock market contributes to the efficiency of modern capitalist corporations suggests some mechanisms that might offer incentives for the directors to improve their performance and prevent the executive branch of government from changing their appointments so frequently. One possibility would be to give the following rights to minority shareholders:

1. The right to require the majority shareholder to replace the board of directors, or any single director;
2. The power to veto the replacement of the board of directors, or any single director, by the majority shareholder; and
3. The power to establish criteria for remunerating the directors.

Of course, if its decisions were turned down by the minority shareholders under these new mechanisms, the state could react by buying up all the shares on the market. To offset this possibility, the state should be forbidden to increase or exceed a certain level of shareholding participation in these types of corporations.

Conclusion

The failure of the state to regulate the prices of public services is a recurrent fact in Brazil's history. The chief reason for this failure is the lack of an institutional framework that would allow independent regulation, dissociated from short-term economic policies and based on criteria of rationality and economic efficiency.

The evidence of the last twenty years shows that the criteria established for the government's pricing policy were not complied with in practice and that the agencies responsible for the regulation lacked the political power to prevent the prices of oil, electrical energy, and telecommunications from being used on many occasions for different purposes and even as instruments of macroeconomic policy in the fight against inflation.

One way to correct the present distortions in price regulation in monopoly sectors of Brazil's economy might be to create a single regulatory agency relatively independent of the executive power, one that would use regulatory instruments, such as price controls and quality standards, to stimulate economic efficiency.

The role of the state as controlling shareholder in corporations of mixed ownership has led to a high turnover rate among their directors and, as a result of the excessive political interference in the administration of these corporations, has at the same time proved incapable of creating mechanisms to encourage economic efficiency.

One way to change this state of affairs might be to introduce modifications into the specific legislation of these corporations to allow minority shareholders greater participation in their administration in order to enhance efficiency and make such enterprises more independent of executive power.

This chapter has analyzed two specific cases of state intervention in Brazil's economy, as regulator of the prices of oil, electrical energy, and telecommunications services and as controlling shareholder in corporations of mixed ownership. In both cases the present institutional framework has been identified as the chief culprit in the inefficiency of state intervention and must be changed. The proposed institutional changes lie within a promarket strategy that can be applied to similar situations in Brazil's economy.

Notes

[1] A. A. Berle and G. C. Means, *The Modern Corporation and Private Property* (London: Macmillan, 1944).

[2] O. E. Williamson, *The Economics of Discretionary Behavior: Managerial Objectives in a Theory of the Firm* (Englewood Cliffs, N.J.: Prentice-Hall, 1964).

Bibliography

Averch, H., and L. Johnson. "Behavior of the Firm under Regulatory Constraint." *American Economic Review* 52 (1962): 1053–69.

Barbosa, F. H., H. L. Arteiro, M. J. L. Caldas, and M. J. Pina. "Aspectos Economicos do Setor Produtivo Estatal no Brasil: Telecomuniçaões, Eletricidade Petróleo." EPGE/Fundação Getúlio Vargas, Rio de Janeiro, 1991. Mimeo.

Baumol, W., and A. Klevorick. "Input Choices and Rate of Return Regulation: An Overview of the Discussion." *The Bell Journal of Economics and Management Science* 1 (1970): 162–90.

Berle, A. A. and G. C. Means. *The Modern Corporation and Private Property*. London: Macmillan, 1944.

Crew, M. A., and P. R. Kleindorfer. *The Economics of Public Utility Regulation*. London: Macmillan, 1986.

Cullis, J. G., and P. R. Jones. *Microeconomics and the Public Economy: A Defence of Leviathan*. Oxford: Basil Blackwell, 1987.

Kahn, A. E. *The Economics of Regulation*. New York: John Wiley. Vol. 1, *Principles* (1970); Vol. 2, *Institutional Issues* (1971).

Rees, R. *Public Enterprise Economics*. 2nd ed. London: Weidenfeld and Nicolson, 1984.

Rees, R. "The Theory of Principal and Agent: Part I and Part II." In J. D. Hey and P. Lambert, eds., *Survey in the Economics of Uncertainty*. Oxford: Basil Blackwell, 1987.

Ross, S. "The Economic Theory of Agency: The Principal's Problem." *American Economic Review* 63 (1973): 134–39.

Williamson, O. E. *The Economics of Discretionary Behavior: Managerial Objectives in a Theory of the Firm*. Englewood Cliffs, N.J.: Prentice-Hall, 1964.

Chapter 5

Industrial Restructuring and Economic Integration: The Outlook for MERCOSUR

José Tavares de Araujo, Jr.

On the day that President Fernando Collor took office, he inaugurated an economic stabilization plan ending most of the administrative controls on imports that had been the foundation of the past decade's regime of indiscriminate protection. Three months later, on June 26, 1990, Collor enacted a program that would gradually reduce customs tariffs through 1994. These measures are, however, only the initial steps toward a broader process of change in the international relations of the Brazilian economy. To guarantee the continuity of this process, the government must first ensure that its trade policy is consistent with its other actions—monetary and fiscal above all. We can gain some crucial insights into the nature of this challenge by examining two topics that will head Brazil's foreign affairs agenda in the coming years: the MERCOSUR project, which is intended to create a common market among Southern Cone economies, and former president Bush's Enterprise for the Americas Initiative, which is intended to establish a free trade area (FTA) between the United States and Latin America.

The first section of this chapter offers a four-part analysis of the MERCOSUR project. Following a brief introduction, the first part sketches the project background and traces the evolution of talks between Argentina and Brazil from the 1986 protocols to the Buenos Aires Act of July 1990. The second part diagnoses the limitations and prospects of the Treaty of Asunción, which in March 1991 created the MERCOSUR project. The third part discusses the problem of exchange rate instability and suggests an interim solution, applicable until the region overcomes its inflationary pressures. The fourth part considers the disparate levels of efficiency displayed by MERCOSUR economies as well as the mechanisms that might keep these imbalances from becoming bulwarks of resistance to the process of integration.

The second section of the chapter examines the links between the MERCOSUR project and the Bush initiative. Two topics are underscored: bilateral trade negotiations between Brazil and the United States, and the multilateral problems the Bush initiative or anything like it may encounter in the foreign exchange arena. There is a summary of the chapter's main conclusions on page 117.

MERCOSUR: Background and Prospects

Because it involves the largest economy in the region, Brazil's trade policy exerts a strong influence on Latin America's economic prospects. However, one of the singularities of its industrialization process has been a tendency for Brazil's economy increasingly to grow apart from the economies of its neighbors. We can distinguish two components within this process of separation: one involving the formulation of investment plans and the other involving the enforcement of policies to control the balance of payments.

A good share of Brazil's productive capacity in capital goods and basic inputs was installed during the past twenty years. The investment plans that laid the foundations for these sectors arose from a strategy that ignored the supply potential of similar industries in neighboring nations. One consequence was to foster inefficient industrial structures composed of firms that are overdiversified or overintegrated vertically; this in turn led to inadequate product mixes, given available technology. Another consequence was the elimination of potential intraindustry trade among the region's economies.

Furthermore, when exchange rate crises forced Brazil to apply import restrictions, the government failed to grant Latin American nations differential treatment—and that generated needless costs. Witness the experience of the first half of the 1980s: between 1981 and 1985 Brazil's trade with members of ALADI (Latin American Integration Association) plummeted from US$7.4 billion to US$3.8 billion in current dollars. While Brazil managed to obtain sizable trade surpluses elsewhere around the world, its exports to all ALADI member nations dropped in almost the same proportion as imports. In terms of the balance of payments, this policy was merely inept, but in terms of income and employment, it effectively aggravated the recession at home and spread it thoughout the continent.

The data provided in Figures 5.1, 5.2, and 5.3 and Table 5.1 bear out these observations. According to CEPAL (United Nations Economic Commission for Latin America and the Caribbean) estimates, in 1989 Brazil's GDP was 37.5 percent of Latin America's total.[1] Throughout that same decade Brazil's trade with Latin America held steady at 40 to 50 percent of intraregional trade despite the nation's protectionist policies, exchange rate instability, and other components of the 1980s crisis (see Figure 5.1). However, as Figure 5.2 illustrates, over the past twenty years the region has had little importance for Brazil, representing from 10 to 17 percent of the nation's trade volume.

If the current trade policy were supplemented by exchange rate stability, the picture drawn by Figures 5.1 and 5.2 would

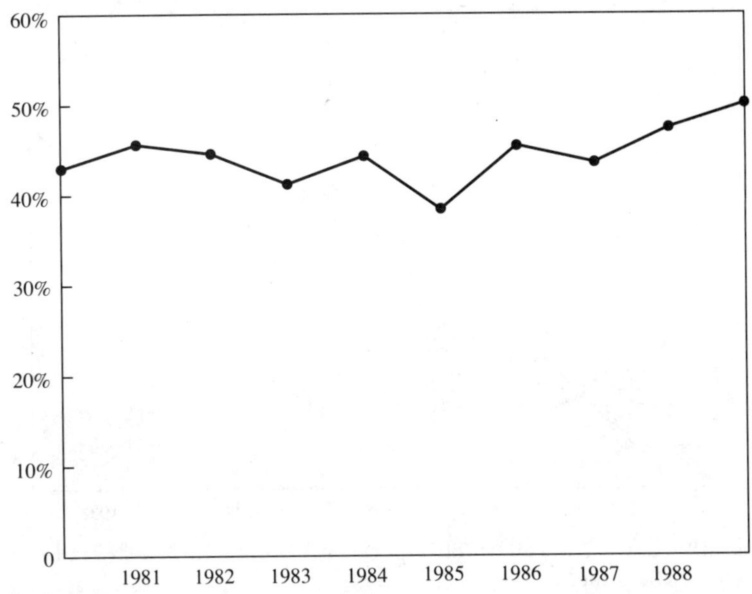

FIGURE 5.1 Brazil's Trade with Latin America as a Share of All Trade within Latin America.
SOURCE: CACEX (Foreign Trade Office, Bank of Brazil)

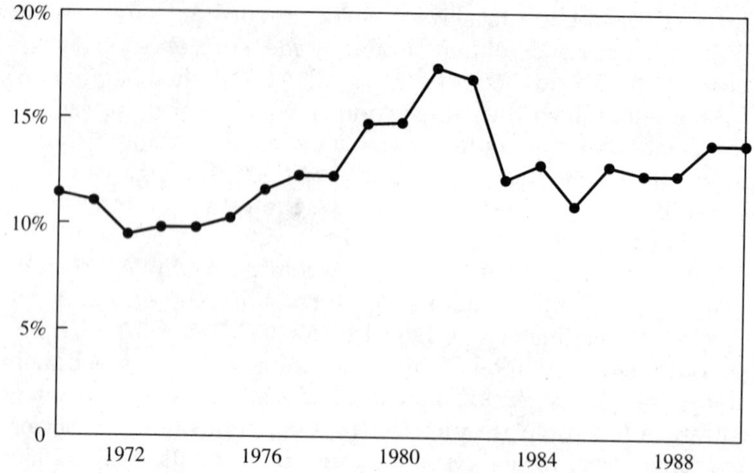

FIGURE 5.2 The Percentage of Latin American Trade in Brazil's Total Foreign Trade.
SOURCE: CACEX (Foreign Trade Office, Bank of Brazil)

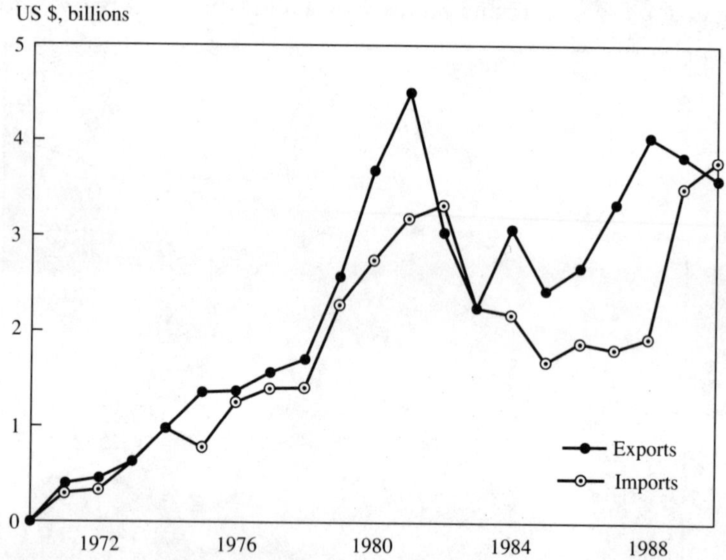

FIGURE 5.3 The Pattern of Imports and Exports in Brazil's Trade with Latin America.
SOURCE: CACEX (Foreign Trade Office, Bank of Brazil)

TABLE 5.1
BRAZIL'S MAIN TRADING
PARTNERS IN LATIN AMERICA
(Percentage of Brazil's Latin American Trade)

	1970	1975	1980	1985	1990
Argentina	54.3	29.2	28.6	24.7	28.0
Chile	8.0	9.6	13.8	11.0	13.4
Mexico	5.8	11.0	14.0	14.6	9.6
Paraguay	2.0	6.8	7.8	9.2	9.6
Uruguay	7.2	8.0	7.9	6.8	12.2
Others	22.7	35.4	27.9	33.7	27.2

SOURCE: CACEX (Foreign Trade Office, Bank of Brazil).

rise remarkably. Given the relative size of the Brazilian economy, its imports have a strong impact on overall transactions within the region. As seen in Figure 5.3, from 1970 through 1990 Brazil's export performance within Latin America was a direct function of its import performance. In fact, during that twenty-year period, on only two occasions—once, in 1975, following the first oil shock and again, in 1988–1989, when the cruzeiro was overvalued within the region—did imports rise without a corresponding growth in exports. Trade diversification is also an important factor, as illustrated in Table 5.1. During the 1980s, 40 percent to 50 percent of Brazil's trade transactions with Latin America involved the other MERCOSUR economies (Argentina, Paraguay, and Uruguay), while about 25 percent involved Chile and Mexico and from 27.2 percent to 33.7 percent involved all other nations in the region.

FROM THE PROTOCOLS OF 1986 TO THE BUENOS AIRES ACT

The trade volume recovery that took place in the second half of the 1980s, reflected in Figures 5.1 through 5.3, was thanks in large part to the set of bilateral protocols signed by President Raúl Alfonsín of Argentina and President José Sarney of Brazil from 1986 to 1990 with the purpose of promoting the economic integration of their countries.

These protocols had two major immediate goals and one long-term goal. In the short run, they were supposed to recover the early-1980s level of transactions and correct systematic imbalances in the flow of trade from the first half of the 1980s. In the long run, they were intended to mold a new pattern of relations between the two economies—one that would provide a firm foundation for growth in the region. To this end, the protocols defined a varied agenda of measures: the strengthening of trade preferences, the removal of nontariff barriers, and the introduction of new projects involving technological cooperation, integrated programs in sectors such as capital goods and wheat, and mechanisms for the financing of trade promotion.

The signing of these protocols was accompanied by an ample revision of both nations' trade ties with Uruguay. Bilateral talks led to the broadening of Argentina and Uruguay's economic cooperation agreement (CAUCE) and of Brazil and Uruguay's trade expansion program (PEC). These agreements exempted nearly all of Uruguay's exportable supply from import taxes and other barriers.

Some of the results of these measures can be seen in Table 5.2, which shows the evolution of Brazil's trade with Argentina and Uruguay from 1980 to 1988.

The most significant impact was on Brazil's exchange with Uruguay, where bilateral trade climbed some 130 percent between 1985 and 1988. Achievements in relation to Argentina were more modest. Although trade grew by 40 percent during the first year of the integration program, this performance was not repeated in following years; instead it held steady at around US$1.4 billion until 1987, rising to US$1.7 billion in 1988.

Despite this relative success, a number of specific measures did not have the desired effects. After 1986, for example, Brazil's wheat imports sank below 1984–1985 levels, although the object of the protocol had been to expand them. The capital goods protocol—one of the program's hallmarks—also fell short of initial expectations.[2] This protocol defined a set of mechanisms to regulate balanced expansion of bilateral trade in equipment. Instruments for trade promotion would be applied to a negotiated list of goods to be treated as "national products" on both sides of the border and thus not subject to protectionist restraint. In 1988, after three years of negotiations, the trade value of the list represented only US$353 million, whereas in 1980 it had stood at US$431 million. In fact, although capital goods trade with

Uruguay enjoyed no special incentive, it proved more dynamic during this period.

Still, the 1986 protocols reaped an invaluable political reward: an unprecedented climate of harmonious, cooperative relations between Brazil and Argentina, which replaced an age-old tradition of rivalry and mistrust.[3]

Flexibility and pragmatism were two catchwords that dominated official discourse the year the integration program was inaugurated. They were used to justify a lack of defined deadlines or concrete commitments to policy harmonization in the common market project. This apparent inconsistency between means and ends was due to the audacious stabilization programs just inaugurated by Argentina and Brazil—the Austral and Cruzado plans, respectively. At least in the first moments of their national experiments, neither government wished to make the pace of bilateral integration contingent on domestic policy performance.

This strategy of balancing integration with domestic goals was short-lived, however. For Brazil, it forced such juggling acts as attempting to reconcile generalized protectionism of local production with full free trade relations with Argentina, while forfeiting any discussion of the partner's trade policy. In Argentina, it meant that local industry would have to begin competing with Brazilian producers who enjoyed a much greater array of government favors.

Hence, whenever the goals of Brazilian or Argentinian domestic policy conflicted in the short run with the objectives of integration, home-front concerns won out. It was impossible to boost Brazil's imports of wheat, for example, because the Brazilian government did not modify its system of agricultural subsidies. Furthermore, the collapse of the Austral and Cruzado plans, and the consequent worsening of inflationary crises in both countries, dried up investments that should have sustained the growth of trade in capital goods.

Despite these vicissitudes, and in an effort to preserve the venture's political gains, Alfonsín and Sarney sought to consolidate the negotiations carried out during their administrations by signing a binational treaty in November 1988—the Buenos Aires Act—stipulating a ten-year deadline for creation of the common market. Ratified by both nations' congresses in August 1989, the integration program went from an absence of policy harmonization to a strong commitment to such harmonization. According

TABLE 5.2

BRAZIL'S TRADE WITH OTHER SOUTHERN CONE ECONOMIES (1980–1988)
(US$ Millions)

	Brazilian imports								
	From Argentina					From Uruguay			
Year	Wheat	Other farm products	Capital goods	Other goods	Total	Farm products	Industrial inputs	Other goods	Total
1980	172	266	74	245	757	39	82	75	196
1981	9	202	59	317	587	33	83	62	176
1982	39	260	41	210	550	49	102	0	151
1983	0	147	26	185	358	53	76	2	131
1984	104	134	35	238	511	34	65	24	123
1985	105	89	47	226	469	47	80	13	140
1986	84	235	62	356	737	94	143	64	301
1987	98	137	91	249	575	42	136	68	246
1988	97	198	113	299	707	69	170	75	314

Brazilian exports

Year	To Argentina				To Uruguay			
	Consumer goods	Capital goods	Industrial inputs	Total	Consumer goods	Capital goods	Industrial inputs	Total
1980	214	357	521	1,092	51	150	109	310
1981	163	269	446	880	50	198	125	373
1982	93	114	460	667	32	48	58	138
1983	76	165	413	654	21	26	57	104
1984	123	171	559	853	26	34	76	136
1985	88	140	320	548	25	48	67	140
1986	130	170	382	682	28	72	103	203
1987	101	252	478	831	32	126	109	267
1988	81	240	658	979	41	131	149	321

SOURCE: CACEX (Foreign Trade Office, Bank of Brazil).

to Article 4, the following policies would be adjusted during the 1990s: "customs, domestic and foreign trade, agricultural, industrial, transportation and communications, scientific and technological, and others to which the two nations agree." The text goes on to state that "furthermore, monetary, fiscal, exchange, and capital policies shall be gradually coordinated under specific Agreements, which, in the corresponding cases, shall be approved by the legislative body of the Federative Republic of Brazil and by the legislative body of the Republic of Argentina."

At their first meeting, on July 6, 1990, President Collor of Brazil and President Menem of Argentina underscored their endorsement of the integration policy, taking three steps meant to hasten the pace of the treaty before it had even gone into effect: they scheduled the date of project conclusion for December 31, 1994, a full four years earlier than the original deadline; they agreed that tariff reductions would be linear and generalized; and they signed the Treaty on Binational Enterprises.

The last two of these measures most certainly were important advances. For one thing, replacing product-by-product negotiations with linear tariff cuts did away with a source of dissimulated resistance to integration; that is, that group of businessmen who applauded the project in generic terms but sought to keep their own products off the trade preference lists. Secondly, the Treaty on Binational Enterprises enhanced a process that is vital to the creation of a common market: the convergence of economic agents' interests. The treaty guarantees that firms whose majority stock lies in Argentinian or Brazilian hands will be treated as national firms on both sides of the border. The many advantages gained include access to official credit instruments, to any and all types of government incentive or subsidy, and to government purchases. Besides stimulating the growth and diversification of transactions between the two economies, these binational companies exert additional pressure in favor of integration whenever they defend their interests through business organizations or in the media.

All the same, the decision to shorten the program deadline was foolhardy. In view of the differences between the two nations' governmental apparatuses and the magnitude of their current macroeconomic imbalances, it will be impossible to thoroughly harmonize economic policies within four years, as announced. Europe itself, unhampered by inflationary or foreign debt crises, spent more than three decades working out its unification process and even now faces serious difficulties. Brazil and Argentina's hurry-up attitude has been a pointless attempt to protect the project's credibility by keeping it in the headlines. It is also a repetition of innumerable other efforts that have in the past helped to discredit the idea of Latin American integration—a proposal that has for decades been a victim of inconsequential government rhetoric.

The Treaty of Asunción

Its unrealistic goals notwithstanding, the Buenos Aires Act was ratified and broadened on March 26, 1991, when Paraguay and Uruguay signed the Treaty of Asunción. This agreement states that a Southern Cone common market, or MERCOSUR, would be created by 1994.

In addition to the commitments under the Buenos Aires Act, the Treaty of Asunción provides for (1) the free circulation of goods, services, and productive factors between these nations and (2) the harmonization of pertinent laws and regulations to ensure the achievement of the first goal.

Although the MERCOSUR project cannot possibly become a reality within the announced time frame, it could be feasible to create an FTA in 1994 if the governments of Argentina and Brazil achieve the feat of stabilizing their economies by that time. To elaborate on this suggestion, we must first have a clear understanding of the differences between two processes: trade liberalization and market unification.

Strictly speaking, a trade liberalization effort consists solely of implementing a GATT rule known as the national treatment principle. As Richard Lipsey and Murray Smith have argued:

> This principle allows the . . . countries to have widely divergent domestic policies. Under a national treatment obligation, a country undertakes to ensure that foreign and domestic producers will be subject to the same laws and regulations in its domestic market. There is no requirement that foreign producers receive the same treatment abroad as they receive in their home market.[4]

In short, to save MERCOSUR from joining the ranks of Latin America's past failures, it would be advisable, while there is still time, to temporarily reduce the scope of MERCOSUR to that of a free trade treaty and to fix more sensible deadlines for the formation of a common market. In this form the program would concentrate on finding solutions to two types of problems: exchange rate instability and the disparate levels of efficiency displayed by the productive structures of the treaty nations.

EXCHANGE RATE INSTABILITY: PART ONE

Figures 5.4, 5.5, and 5.6 depict the quarterly evolution of real cruzeiro exchange rates against MERCOSUR nation currencies over the past twenty years.

Except for Uruguay, where reasonable stability can be observed between 1975 and 1979 (Figure 5.5), all other data reveal not only erratic imbalances but also quite heterogenous intervals of oscillation. For example, from 1971 to 1973 the cruzeiro was falling against the austral (then the Argentine peso), rising against the Uruguayan peso and holding steady in relation to the Paraguayan guarani. During the first quarter of 1975 the cruzeiro was strong against the austral, weak against the guarani, and relatively steady against the Uruguayan peso. In fact, if we take any stretch during this two-decade period, we

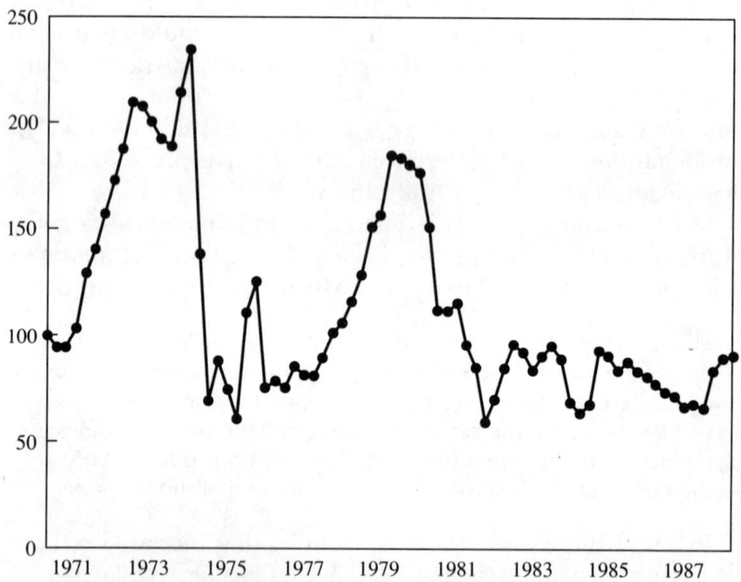

FIGURE 5.4 Exchange Rates for the Brazilian Cruzeiro against the Argentinian Austral.

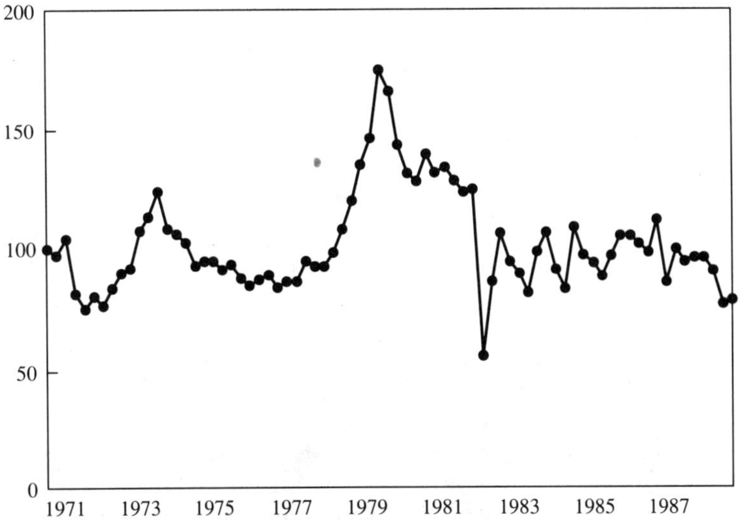

FIGURE 5.5 Exchange Rates for the Brazilian Cruzeiro against the Uruguayan Peso.

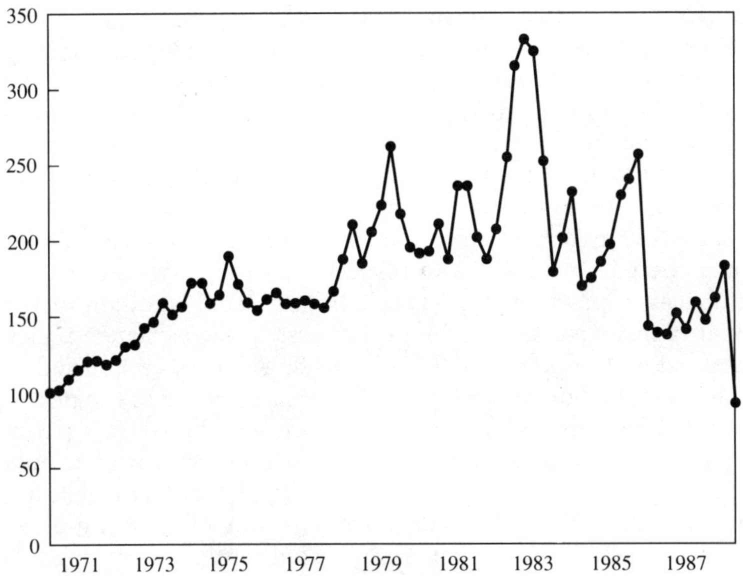

FIGURE 5.6 Exchange Rates for the Brazilian Cruzeiro against the Paraguayan Guarani.

will detect such asymmetry. By the same token, exchange rate maximums and minimums differed by some 120 percentage points in the case of the Uruguayan peso, 180 in the case of the austral, and 240 in the case of the guarani.[5]

Enduring instability of such magnitude has made it infeasible to maintain stronger ties between these economies. At any given moment, one currency may be overvalued against another. Capital flow from the "strong" currency nation will then generate exceptional revenue for investors, but in compensation, exports from the other nation—the one with the "weak" currency—will become more competitive within the neighboring country's market. Because the circumstances may suddenly reverse themselves (and because the economic agents are already used to this), only those deals not requiring long-term commitments will be closed.

This problem derives to a great extent from dissimilarities in the region's inflationary processes during these two decades. As Table 5.3 indicates, each of the four economies has its own particular history of price evolution. Argentina, which has been grappling with three-digit annual inflation rates since 1975, reached a hyperinflationary pinnacle in 1989–1990. Brazil, albeit on somewhat the same path, managed to hold its inflation down to two digits throughout the 1970s. Paraguay, on the other hand, experienced inflation rates of over 30 percent only in 1986 and 1990, while Uruguay reached three digits for the first time in 1990, having earlier gone through phases both of rising inflation, at the beginning of the 1970s and between 1983 and 1990, and of downward rates, as in the 1979–1982 period.

Other sources of exchange rate instability are the myriad exchange controls that Latin American governments have adopted over the past forty years to respond to disequilibrium in their balances of payments. In each nation the sophistication of the control instruments and the explicitness of the exchange policy depend on the power wielded by those segments interested in the overvaluation of the local currency as opposed to the power wielded by those who stand to gain from exchange rate parity or devaluation. The former group basically comprises agents involved in import activities, whose domestic market profits are an increasing function of currency overvaluation. This group's allies usually include government authorities who, regardless of how big the economy's ratio of imports to GDP (import

TABLE 5.3
ANNUAL RATES OF INFLATION
IN SOUTHERN CONE ECONOMIES

Year	Argentina	Brazil	Paraguay	Uruguay
1970	13.6	17.0	−0.7	17.0
1971	34.8	21.1	4.8	24.0
1972	58.4	17.8	9.5	76.5
1973	61.2	15.5	12.5	97.0
1974	23.5	34.5	25.2	77.2
1975	182.3	29.4	6.8	81.4
1976	443.2	46.3	4.6	50.6
1977	176.1	38.8	9.3	58.2
1978	175.5	40.8	10.6	44.5
1979	159.5	77.2	28.3	66.8
1980	100.8	110.2	22.4	63.5
1981	104.5	95.2	14.0	34.0
1982	164.8	99.7	6.8	19.0
1983	343.8	211.0	13.4	49.2
1984	626.7	233.8	20.3	55.3
1985	672.1	235.1	25.2	77.2
1986	90.1	65.0	31.7	76.4
1987	131.3	415.8	21.8	63.6
1988	343.0	1,037.6	24.5	62.2
1989	3,079.3	1,782.9	26.2	80.4
1990	1,832.5	1,476.6	42.7	129.8

SOURCE: International Monetary Fund, *International Financial Statistics*, various editions.

coefficient), are often willing to underwrite a trade-off between delayed realignment of the exchange rate and artificial results in the war against inflation. Conversely, the strength of the adversary group depends not only on the relative size of the sector comprising exporters and producers of goods that compete with imports, but also the extent to which the economy is integrated into the international finance system.

Because this battle of interests takes a distinct form in each country, exchange rate policies naturally vary from nation to nation within the region. To reach a definitive solution to this problem, these countries must end inflation and adopt macroeconomic policies that will make price stability as high a priority as exchange rate stability. But this is not the most likely scenario for either Argentina or Brazil in the near future. It would be wise—

if the MERCOSUR project is to survive—to create a mechanism that will at least ensure a measure of parity among the region's currencies until it is possible to begin effectively harmonizing exchange rate policies.

This mechanism would entail the following measures:

1. The agreement already signed by Brazil and Argentina would be enforced; that is, regional transactions would be recorded in *gauchos,* a regional currency created by the 1986 protocols, whose value is equal to one IMF Special Drawing Right.
2. Each government would hold the purchasing power of its currency steady against the gaucho. In practice, this would most likely produce a double, or multiple, exchange rate system, depending on the prevailing policies of each nation.
3. To avoid generating systematic imbalances within the region, each government would endeavor to adjust its national policies to ensure parity with the gaucho; and
4. The issuance of gauchos would be the responsibility of a committee composed of the four nations' central banks. This same body would deal with disequilibrium in the intraregional balance of payments. Considering the heterogeneous sizes of the economies involved, it would be best to develop criteria that would allow creditors and debtors to share the costs of adjustment, but within strict limits that would forestall any new source of inflation, in heed of Daniel Cohen's word of warning.[6]

Introducing dual exchange rates to achieve monetary stability is not a new idea. In analyzing the performance of the European monetary system (EMS), Tommaso Padoa-Schioppa cautioned that the system could evolve toward an "inconsistent quartet" of policies, encompassing (1) free trade, (2) full capital mobility, (3) fixed exchange rates, and (4) national autonomy in conducting monetary policy.[7] To avert this risk, Dornbusch suggested that the EMS use two exchange rates, one for current transactions and the other for capital flow.[8]

In the medium run, this exchange rate system could ensure the continuity of two interlinked processes. First, within the sphere of MERCOSUR, the proposed system would move gradually toward overall harmonization of exchange rate policies and eventually of other policies as well, as the region's economies gained greater stability. Second, once the initial version of the system were proven effective, other Latin American nations would be stimulated to participate, thereby triggering a kind of interaction between MERCOSUR and the rest of the region similar to the present relationship between the European Economic Community (EEC) and the European Free Trade Association (EFTA). Although EFTA's member nations do not formally participate in the EMS, they arrange their exchange policies in accordance with parameters defined under the latter system.[9]

Disparities in Productivity

Although the Buenos Aires Act created a process that would automatically reduce trade barriers among members of the MERCOSUR project, no way has yet been found to prevent disparities in the efficiency of productive systems from hindering integration.[10]

Given the current state of these economies, two types of measures would be feasible. The primary objective of the first measure would be to rigidly compartmentalize talks so that the peculiarities of the agricultural sector (such as seasonality, crop failure, and overproduction) could not be used to obstruct progress in other areas. It would initially suffice to set up a coordinating and consulting forum that included the agriculture ministers of the MERCOSUR nations. Their main duties would be to evaluate the regional outlook for production and supply each semester and recommend adjustments in price policies, subsidies, intraregional trade, and trade with third markets. In the long run, this forum would tend to consolidate as the body responsible for planning and executing a common agricultural policy for the region, as in Europe.

The second measure would be aimed basically at the industrial sector, although it might also benefit such areas as communications, transportation, and infrastructure. The idea would be to hasten adaptation of the Treaty on Binational Enterprises signed by Argentina and Brazil into the MERCOSUR framework and to use the experience and resources of Brazil's national development bank, the BNDES, in collaboration with finance agencies from the other nations, to introduce a program that would support ventures related to economic integration. In practice, this program would simply extend to the regional project some of the lines of finance that the BNDES has been operating in Brazil for a number of years now, for example, those covering the expansion of productive capacity, mergers and acquisitions, R&D projects, and the purchase of technology.

The Enterprise for the Americas Initiative: Negotiation Strategies and Exchange Rate Stability

The creation of an FTA between the United States and Latin America would have two main consequences for the foreign relations of the Brazilian economy. In bilateral terms it would represent a new milestone in addressing trade disputes with the U.S. government. In regional terms it would force the Brazilian government to confront three issues: meeting the goals of the MERCOSUR project, complying with the commitments signed within ALADI, and engaging in multilateral negotiations between nations in the region and the United States.

During the 1980s the key points of contention between Brazil and the United States were Brazilian laws and regulations regarding pharmaceutical patents, Brazil's reserving its computer information market to Brazilian companies, and U.S. protectionism in the steel, textile, footwear, and orange juice industries. A number of the items on this agenda would be immediately reviewed or simply eliminated under the Bush initiative. Some have in fact already been altered since the advent of the Collor administration.

The trade controversies between Brazil and the United States, however, are still fueled by two kinds of disequilibria that will be corrected only through lengthier talks. First, a certain set of Brazilian industries boasts plants that are much more competitive than their U.S. counterparts, because of factors such as the diffusion of innovation, the technological vintage of facilities, and the level of labor costs. The remedy for this imbalance is widely known but hard to swallow, by virtue of the unequal distribution of the costs involved in industrial restructuring. On the other hand, the inverse situation can be found concentrated in high-tech industries. Here there are no consensus solutions, not only because of clashing views on the most suitable form and content of a technology policy for an economy like Brazil's, but also because of the countless competitive strategies available to holders of limited-access technologies. An analysis of these two types of conflict and the possible ways around them is the topic of the following section.

As to Brazil's economic relations with the remainder of Latin America, it should first of all be noted that the Bush initiative, the MERCOSUR project, and other integration efforts underway in the region can perfectly well converge. Proof of this is the history of relations between the EEC and the EFTA. Each EFTA member (Austria, Finland, Iceland, Norway, Sweden, and Switzerland) has signed a bilateral agreement with the EEC, in addition to the multilateral treaty maintained among EFTA members. These eight protocols—six bilateral agreements; the Treaty of Rome, which created the EEC; and the EFTA statutes—have been working smoothly for many years now.[11] However, as Francesco Giavazzi and Alberto Giovannini have shown, the secret behind this success is Europe's stubborn stance on exchange rate stability.[12] One of the dilemmas that the Bush initiative or NAFTA would create for Latin America would be whether to choose automatic alignment to the dollar or some other stabilization mechanisms. This issue is examined later in the chapter.

It may be helpful to warn that the present study intends to discuss neither the motivations behind the Bush initiative, nor the likelihood of its actual enforcement, nor even its potential impact on Latin American economies. Instead we will focus on the terms and conditions that would be imposed on Brazilian trade policy at the outset of the creation of a U.S.–Latin American FTA.

Competitiveness and Protectionism

In a previous work I showed that in a context of exchange rate stability, some 85 percent to 90 percent of Brazil's installed productive capacity could compete with imported goods, with the support of the tariff structure the government intends to enact by 1994.[13] The country's current competitiveness profile reveals three different kinds of situations. Some areas, such as pulp, petrochemicals, and specialty steels, continue to operate according to international standards of quality and technical efficiency, despite disturbances born of a decade of macroeconomic instability. Other areas, like capital goods and machine tools, are now losing their competitiveness of the early 1980s but could easily recoup it if the economy's medium-term outlook were better. But sectors like computers and the information industry (informatics) and biotechnology would be able to keep march with international technical progress only if they could count on government support.

Against the background of the current economic picture in the United States, Brazil's competitiveness profile should elicit the following discussion points in the event of bilateral talks toward a free trade agreement:

1. Competitive industries whose exports do not trigger protectionist demands by other nations;
2. Industries of diffused innovations that in one nation have a competitive edge over their sister companies in another nation; and
3. High-tech industries.

Industries in category 1 include segments of foodstuffs, agricultural machinery, and pulp in Brazil; photographic material and scientific instruments in the United States; and aircraft industry components and auto parts in both nations. These industries would be among the first to be governed by free trade terms. The scope of talks would in this case be limited to the order in which sectors should be included in the agreement and deadlines for abolishing trade barriers.

Steel, textiles, and footwear in Brazil and electrical appliances and telecommunications equipment in the United States are some examples of category 2 industries. Here, liberalization should be accompanied by measures to eliminate disparities in competitiveness. More important than negotiating deadlines for the correction of inequalities, however, would be developing acceptable interim forms of protection. The recent history of protectionism suggests two principles useful in approaching this topic. The first is that every type of protection has its price, inasmuch as it transfers rents to protected sectors. The second is that related costs are borne differently by local consumers and by the industries of trading partners, depending on the type of protection instrument adopted. Thus, it is possible to choose instruments that do not conflict with the goal of expanding trade, as long as the bill is footed solely by local consumers.

Two kinds of protection are usually applied to high-tech industries (category 3), whose most popular examples today are informatics, biotechnology, fine chemicals, and precision mechanics such as the repair of airplanes and computers. The countries that were the cradles of these innovations have protected their industries by erecting barriers not against the trading of final goods but against the diffusion of knowledge of relevant production techniques. The protectionist policies of other nations consist of a combination of conventional instruments (such as import taxes and quotas, government procurement, and subsidies) to assist infant industries, at times adopted in conjunction with restrictions on foreign investments and with policies aimed at the acquisition of technological skills.

If this item of the agenda is to be negotiable, there must be a consensus on certain general principles. First, the holders of technology must be remunerated for their investments in research and development, but they cannot be allowed to explicitly or covertly hinder access to any of the knowledge inherent to their innovations. Additionally, the protection of infant industries cannot be allowed to obstruct the international dissemination of innovations produced in other countries.

Because technical progress is constantly recreating unequal conditions of competition on a world level, the key point to be agreed upon in discussing categories 2 and 3 is the inevitability of interim protection measures, whose onus must fall solely on the nation adopting such measures. This criterion is recognized in Article 19 of GATT, which addresses the question of safeguards. As is well known, this article has never been adequately applied because GATT members have never been able to agree on instruments that would be acceptable under such circumstances. This is because efficient safeguards usually conflict with the most-favored-nation principle and the exclusiveness of tariffs as protection instruments.

Herein lies one of the greatest challenges to the negotiators of this agreement. Much as the agreement between Canada and the United States accelerated GATT talks on service and investment themes, the success of the Enterprise for the Americas Initiative or NAFTA will to a certain extent depend on the ability of its executors to solve the safeguard dilemma.

Exchange Rate Instability: Part Two

Exchange rate stability is a basic prerequisite of a unified economic space, as demonstrated by the role of the EMS in the evolution of the EEC this past decade. It was only in 1986, after six years of actual experience with the new exchange rate rules, that EEC governments felt ready to inaugurate the Europe '92 project. Completing what was initiated in 1958 by the Treaty of Rome, this new proposal abolished all restrictions on the movement of citizens, goods, and capital within the EEC as of January 1, 1993.

Even when the goal is to form an FTA rather than a common market, exchange rate stability still has an essential function, that of reducing the degree of uncertainty in international transactions. With uncertainty reduced, trade flow tends to become more regular, thanks to an increasing number of long-term contracts for the routine supply of goods and services.

For the Bush initiative to have met this requirement, the natural solution would in principle be to peg the region's currencies to the dollar, as the Argentine government has recently done. But this approach has some disadvantages. For example, some countries may not want to align their exchange rates with the dollar, as is well illustrated by the Canadian government's decision to maintain an independent exchange policy in spite of its free trade agreement with the United States.

The ground rules for a fixed exchange rate system were defined in the following terms by an ex-president of the Bundesbank, Otmar Emminger: "A system of fixed rates can only function so long as the key-currency country, by its domestic stability—that is, monetary stability and economic stability in general—enables the other member countries to maintain fixed exchange rates without imposing undue strains on their own domestic stability."[14]

Emminger's definition clarifies the dilemma engendered by the Bush initiative. The problem can be summed up in three points:

1. The Federal Reserve System failed once before to anchor a fixed rate system—that of Bretton Woods—precisely because it did not satisfy the conditions we have discussed;
2. The U.S. government is unlikely to submit its monetary and fiscal policies to the consideration of the other nations on the continent, as is the procedure among EMS members; and
3. No other central bank in the region has strong enough credibility to anchor the system, with the exception of Canada's—and Canada, like the United States, is not interested in adjusting its economic policies to those of Latin American economies.

Until this picture changes, the exchange rate approach suggested in "Exchange Rate Instability: Part One" could be used to create a hybrid system that would peg the rates of Latin American currencies to the cruzeiro, which would in turn float against the dollar.

Conclusion

MERCOSUR and the Enterprise for the Americas Initiative are in different phases of maturation. MERCOSUR, however unrealistic its deadlines, is the result of five years of negotiations and will stall only if the Argentine and Brazilian economies fail to overcome their current crises during this decade. The Bush initiative is as yet only a generic proposal, although it became a reference point for the conduct of Latin American governments.

As I have shown, both projects are subject to the same types of constraints: exchange rate instability and the competitiveness profiles of the economies involved. In wrestling with these issues, it is not enough for the Brazilian government merely to devise adequate negotiating strategies; what is imperative, above all, is at least a minimum degree of consistency in domestic policy.

Notes

1 See the *Statistical Yearbook for Latin America and the Caribbean* (Santiago: CEPAL, 1990), 183.

2 F. Porta, "As Duas Etapas do Programa de Integração Argentina-Brasil: Uma Análise dos Principais Protocolos," in Motta Veiga, ed., *Cone Sul: A Economia Política de Integração* (Rio de Janeiro: FUNCEX, 1991).

3 M. Hirst, "Contexto e Estrategia do Programma de Integraçõ Argentina-Brasil," *Revista de Economia Política* 8 (June 1988); M. Hirst, *El Programa de Integración y Cooperación Argentina-Brazil: Los Nuevos Horizontes de Vinculación Economica y Complementación Industrial,* Serie de Documentos y Informes de Investigación no. 81 (Buenos Aires: FLASCO, 1989).

4 R. Lipsey and M. Smith, "An Introductory Overview," in *Policy Harmonization: The Effects of a Canadian/American Free Trade Area* (Toronto: C.D. Howe Institute, 1986), ix.

5 Notice the volatility of the exchange rates. Figure 5.4 does not record rates for the austral during Argentina's 1989–1990 bout with hyperinflation.

6 D. Cohen, "The Costs and Benefits of a European Currency," in M. De Cecco and A. Giovannini, eds., *A European Central Bank?: Perspective on Monetary*

Unification after Ten Years of the EMS (Cambridge, U.K.: Cambridge University Press, 1989).

[7] T. Padoa-Schioppa, "The European Monetary System: A Long Term View," in F. Giavazzi, S. Micossi, and M. Miller, eds., *The European Monetary System* (Cambridge, U.K.: Cambridge University Press, 1988).

[8] R. Dornbusch, "The European Monetary System, the Dollar and the Yen," in F. Giavazzi, S. Micossi, and M. Miller, eds., *The European Monetary System* (Cambridge, U.K.: Cambridge University Press, 1988).

[9] H. Ungerer, J. Hauvonen, A. Lopez-Claros, and T. Mayer, *The European Monetary System: Developments and Perspectives,* Occasional Paper no. 73 (Washington, D.C., IMF, 1990).

[10] For an analysis of the effects generated by MERCOSUR on the productive structures of member countries, see José Tavares de Araujo, Jr., "Industrial Restructuring and Economic Integration: The Outlook for MERCOSUR," *Revista Brasileira de Economia,* 47, no. 1 (Jan.–March 1993).

[11] V. Curzon-Price, *Free Trade Areas: The European Experience* (Toronto: C.D. Howe Institute, 1987).

[12] F. Giavazzi and A. Giovannini, eds. *Limiting Exchange Rate Flexibility,* (Boston: MIT Press, 1989).

[13] J. T. Araujo, Jr., "*Uma Estratégia nào Liberal para a Abertura da Economia Brasileira,*" Texto para Discusção no. 255 (Rio de Janeiro: IEI/UFRJ, 1991).

[14] O. Emminger, *The D-Mark in the Conflict between Internal and External Equilibrium, 1948–75, Essays on International Finance,* no. 112 (Princeton, N.J.: International Finance Section, Dept. of Economics, Princeton University, 1977). Cited in Giavazzi and Giovannini, *Limiting Exchange Rate Flexibility.*

Chapter 6

Industrial Policy and the Challenge of Competitiveness

Wilson Suzigan

The structure of Brazilian industry expanded and deepened substantially from the mid-1950s to the end of the 1970s. During this period production growth was based on the expansion of the domestic market and the use of remaining investment opportunities of the import substitution industrialization period. Although still insignificant, production for the foreign market rose in importance from the 1970s onward.[1]

The metal-mechanical and chemical industries took on a leading role in the development of Brazilian industry. The most dynamic segments of these industries were the consumer durables and capital goods, which fueled growth in their respective input sectors. Both the weight of those sectors within the industrial structure and the growth they engendered can be attributed to the position of the activities they represent in the nucleus of the international pattern of industrial development with which the Brazilian industrial structure was then converging.[2] Investment absorbed a large amount of the nation's GDP (almost one quarter on yearly average throughout the 1970s) and developed ahead of output. The dynamism of production and investment buoyed industrial productivity, which grew steadily. From 1975 to 1980, for example, productivity (output per person employed or hours worked) in the state of São Paulo rose between 3 percent and 3.5 percent per year, according to data issued by the São Paulo State Federation of Industries (FEISP).

This structure was set up under the shelter of policies that successively and cumulatively favored high levels of generalized permanent protection for domestic industry, with tax and credit subsidies to aid the formation of industrial capital and export incentives and subsidies for industrialized products. Government support for technological development was limited to the acquisition of technological capacity for production, although by the 1970s the institutional foundation for a national system of innovation was already in the early stages of implementation. A science and technology infrastructure had been set up within the federal government as well as the research institutes and universities. In individual companies, however, technological research and development activities—the capacity to innovate—were very limited. Even today Brazilian industry requires broader dissemination of such basic innovations as rigid automation technologies, quality control of products and processes, and standardization and normalization according to the paradigms of electromechanical technologies.

At the end of the 1970s and during the early 1980s Brazil's industrial structure featured high production but insufficient technological development. Specific technical and economic inefficiencies blunted its competitive edge; it also lacked clear-cut specialization standards and was poorly integrated with the international market. This final point is expressed by low import and export coefficients (11 percent and 9 percent respectively for the economy as a whole in 1980 and certainly less for the manufacturing sector). Brazil's international activities reflected the peculiarities of its industrial structure. Its exports tended to consist of natural-resource and energy-intensive goods produced with cheap labor; its imports of technology-intensive goods, particularly machinery, equipment and chemical products.

At the same time the major industrial economies were beginning to introduce innovations in technology, management, and organization that would radically alter the technical foundations of industry along a new pattern of development. The mainstream trend was represented by the new paradigm of information and communication technologies based on microelectronics.

If Brazil were to ensure the continuous upgrading of its own industrial structure, it would clearly need to change the pattern of its industrial and technological development. This would mean incorporating technological, management, and organizational innovations into established industries as well as those developing industries that represent the new technologies.

Only thus could Brazil sustain and increase growth in productivity and employment. But such a breakthough would have required adequate policy changes in industrial, technological, and human resource development. The most necessary changes would have been a reduction in the levels at which the industry would be protected and promoted, and the rationalization of the systems for protection and promotion. The actions and resources of the state and private sectors should have been oriented toward R&D, technological development, and human resource development from basic education to the development of specialized courses.

These changes, however, did not take place. With a few praiseworthy exceptions (as in the development of the informatics industry and the expansion of certain export sectors) the production structure did not change. The macroeconomic instability arising from soaring inflation and the ineffectiveness of a state hamstrung by its own industrial and technological policy—once again, with the exception of the informatics area and isolated initiatives backed by the Ministry of Science and Technology during the second half of the 1980s—led to stagnating industrial output, shrinking investments, and limitations on efforts to incorporate technical progress. The structural configuration that arose from this situation was characterized by marked technological and structural heterogeneity and a weak capacity for innovation. Today these are major hurdles to a return to growth, even with the current pattern of industrial development.

The following two sections discuss the current situation of Brazilian industry, spotlighting its poor performance in production, productivity, investment, and technological development, as well as its structural problems, particularly its technological backwardness and ill-balanced production capacity. Based on this diagnosis, the third section analyzes questions that should guide the formulation of an industrial policy, mainly regarding the degree and timing of liberalization, and assess the extent to which recent government measures in this area have responded to these questions. The closing section presents some final remarks.

Industrial Performance in the 1980s

The adjustments forced on industry by the crisis of the early 1980s interrupted the trends toward increased production and investment prior to 1979, thus weakening the drive of the industrial development pattern previously in force. Some loss of momentum had already been expected as a result of the completion (or partial postponement) of massive blocks of investments launched during the second half of the 1970s intended to expand the production capacity of basic input materials and capital goods. But tough adjustment policies prompted most of the changes from 1981 onward. Levels of production and employment plummeted; productivity waned in 1981 and started to rise again in 1982, but only because employment dropped more sharply than production. Export coefficients rose, thanks to a policy of exports at any cost (on the part of companies and of the federal government, which expanded its subsidies). Such a policy was seen as the answer to the crisis of the domestic market and the tool for generating the trade balances needed to service Brazil's foreign debt. Investment levels eroded more sharply than production shrank, and efforts to incorporate technical progress slowed down, weakening the infrastructure of science and technology that was in its early stages of implementation. We discuss these changes briefly in this section.

THE STAGNATION OF INDUSTRIAL OUTPUT

Taken as a whole, the 1982–1990 period exhibited an utter stagnation of the per capita GDP compared to 1980 levels; by 1990 it had regressed to 1979 levels. Brazil's industrial output also ground to a halt during the 1980s (Figure 6.1). Between 1980 and 1990 real industrial output increased only 3.6 percent, and even this was due to the extraordinary performance of the mining industry (extraction of oil and production of ores for export) and to a few export sectors and the informatics industry then being established.

The manufacturing industry as a whole saw its output shrink by 6.4 percent during this decade. The main sectors responsible for these negative results were capital goods—down 26 percent between 1980 and 1990—and consumer durables, whose 1990 output lagged behind 1980 figures. This trend was in direct opposition to conditions before the crisis, when these categories were at the head of growth tables (Figure 6.2). Sectors in expansion included intermediate goods (3.9 percent over the entire period) and nondurable consumer goods (10.5 percent). The

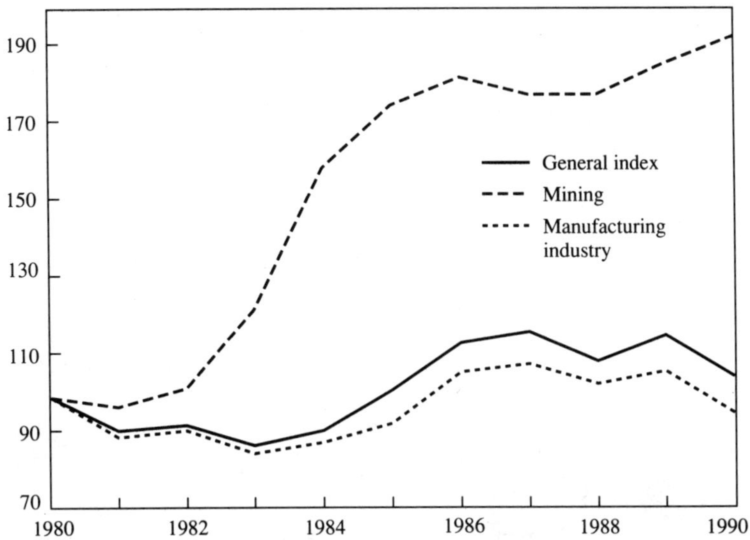

FIGURE 6.1 Indexes of Industrial Production (1980–1990) by Sector.
SOURCE: Brazilian Institute of Geography and Statistics (IBGE—Instituto Brasileiro de Geografia e Estadística).

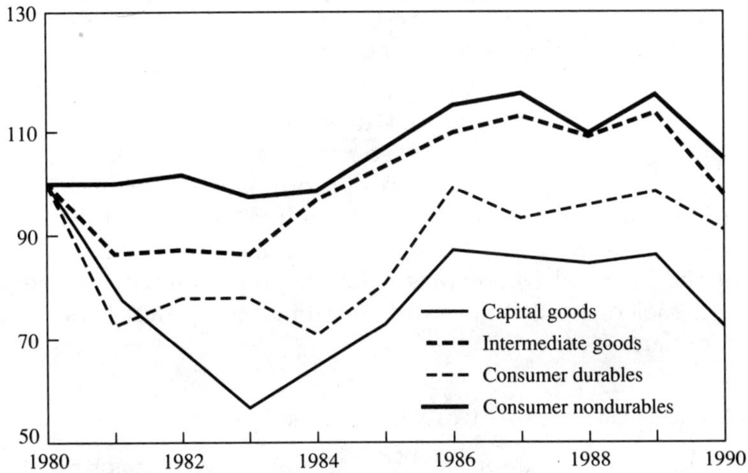

FIGURE 6.2 Indexes of Industrial Production (1980–1990) by Category of Goods.
SOURCE: Brazilian Institute of Geography and Statistics (IBGE—Instituto Brasileiro de Geografia e Estadística).

output of intermediate goods was bolstered by exports, particularly pulp and paper, chemicals and petrochemicals, rubber and tires, and metallurgy. Production of nondurable consumer goods was in its turn fueled by domestic demand of income-inelastic goods such as pharmaceuticals, foodstuffs, beverages, and tobacco. However, other producers of nondurable consumer goods chalked up a negative performance (textiles, clothing, and footwear) despite having channeled an increasing share of their output to the international market. (This poor performance highlights a heavily repressed demand for such goods on the domestic market over the previous ten years.) Among consumer durables, automobile production followed a similar pattern.

It seems clear that changes in sector leadership during the 1980s do not define a new pattern of industrial development. As Sartíand Furtado point out:

> This is not an expansion headed by a new group of activities, inverting certain historical trends. It is rather a phenomenon of a global loss of dynamism, which was avoided—although only partially—in some areas. These are important in terms of their weight in the overall production structure, but are insufficient to provide sustained thrust for growth, due to this weight and their significance in terms of industrial articulation, or their content in terms of the definition of new parameters for industry as a whole.[3]

The only "new" sector that developed, linked to the new paradigm of information and communication technologies, was informatics. However, the task of coordinating Brazil's National Informatics Policy with policies for other segments of the electronic complex, as well as the initial stages in the dismantling of the National Informatics Policy in 1990, limited the range and cooled the dynamism of this timid step toward the new paradigm.

THE REDUCED RATE OF PRODUCTIVITY GROWTH

Trends in industrial productivity also underwent major modification during the 1980s. Although, as we have mentioned, the initial impact of the crisis triggered a collapse in productivity, the fact that employment levels and hours worked decreased even more rapidly than production boosted productivity until the middle of the decade. Output peaked in 1984–85 but was not accompanied by a recovery in employment levels. Indeed, "in 1985, the productivity of the mining and manufacturing industries together was 20.5 percent higher than in 1980, corresponding to an average annual increase of 3.8 percent."[4]

This trend nosedived toward the end of the decade, when a new recession caused production to drop faster than employment, thus engendering a loss in productivity (Figure 6.3). But a concomitant slump in the number of hours worked slowed the productivity decline and even led to an increase of 15.7 percent for 1980–1990. Although these results were appreciable considering the crisis in industry throughout most of the decade, they were mediocre compared to the extraordinary expansion in industrial productivity in the more advanced nations over the same period. Information available for 1980–1987, for example, shows the following increases in industrial productivity by country: Japan 70.5 percent, Belgium 65.4 percent, Italy 58.9 percent, U.K. 48.1 percent, Holland 44.7 percent, France 41.2 percent, Sweden 39.9 percent, United States, West Germany, and Norway 34.2 percent.[5]

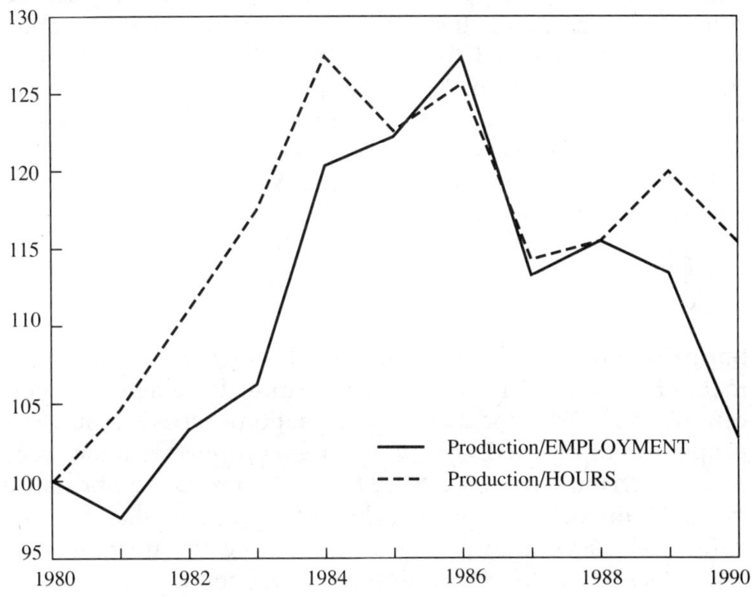

FIGURE 6.3 Productivity Indicators (1980–1990) for São Paulo Industries.

SOURCE: Prepared from primary data supplied by the São Paulo State Federation of Industries (FEISP).

TURNING TO THE INTERNATIONAL MARKET

The most singular characteristic of Brazil's industrial performance from 1981 to 1990 is that a growing portion of output was channeled into the international market. With the end of the large blocks of investment provided by the second National Development Plan (1975–1979), industry ceased to generate its own demand, and possibilities for growth on the domestic market were blocked by the crisis. The international market was thus used as a way out of the crisis in the domestic market rather than an opportunity for corporate expansion. Such expansion did, however, occasionally occur and was, in a few cases, even based on impressive technological advances.

This export boom in industrialized products was heavily concentrated in the metallurgy, machinery, chemicals-petrochemicals, and pulp and paper industrial complexes (Table 6.1). But the boom was also based on the expansion of traditional exports (textiles, clothing, footwear) and rubber products, which represented the *previous* pattern of development, featuring natural resource, energy, and cheap labor-intensive products. Together these factors increased the insertion of Brazilian industry into the international market. This insertion was encouraged by spurious competitive factors: shrinking domestic demand, episodic real devaluations of the Brazilian currency, eroding real wages, strict price controls on the domestic market, and fiscal and credit incentives and subsidies to exports.[6]

SHRINKING INVESTMENTS

Shrinking investments were another strikingly negative benchmark of the 1980s. Having topped an annual average of 24 percent between 1974 and 1980, the formation of fixed capital as a proportion of the GDP (constant prices) dropped to an average of 17.6 percent from 1981 to 1990 as a result of the imbalance in public finances, a reversed flow of foreign capital, and the defensive reactions of private companies to the unstable outlook, sharpened by uncertainty over economic policy and a total lack of industrial and technological policy guidelines. This slippage was most marked in companies owned by the federal government; investments as a proportion of the GDP shriveled from 4.6 percent in 1981 down to 2.3 percent in 1989, largely

TABLE 6.1
SECTOR EXPORTS AS A SHARE OF SECTOR SIZE
AND AS A SHARE OF BRAZIL'S EXPORTS

	Sector exports as a share of sector production 1980	1988	*Sector exports as a share of total exports* 1987–1988
All sectors	10.2%	13.3%	100.0%
Mining	46.0	68.0	6.9
Manufacturing	9.4	11.9	93.1
Selected manufacturing sectors:			
Nonmetallic minerals	2.8	2.9	1.4
Metallurgy	4.7	32.6	14.2
Machinery (nonelectrical)	10.8	10.2	6.3
Electrical and communication material	4.9	8.1	3.2
Transportation material	10.0	17.8	10.0
Paper and cardboard	10.5	13.4	3.4
Rubber	4.9	10.1	1.1
Chemicals	8.8	10.3	15.8
Plastics	1.5	1.0	0.2
Textiles	6.3	10.0	3.3
Clothing and footwear	6.8	26.0	4.4
Foodstuffs	23.8	13.5	19.1
Beverages	7.7	1.6	0.1
Tobacco	29.6	21.8	1.7

SOURCE: F. Sarti and J. Furtado, *Estrutura e Exportacões Industriais nos Anos Oitenta: Elementos para uma Caracterização*, Research Report of the IPT/FECAMP Project "Desenvolvimento Tecnológico da Indústria e a Constituição de um Sistema Nacional de Invacação no Brasil" (Campinas: Institute of Economics, University of Campinas, 1991), 34 and 38.

because of their downgraded self-financing capacities. This in its turn was due to two factors: swelling financial charges arising from the position of these companies as major borrowers of foreign funding since 1978 and outdated prices for public services and goods that dragged on throughout the 1980s.[7] More serious, from the perspective of this study, was that public companies in the industrial sector were hit hardest by this cut in investments—particulary mining (−51.6 percent between 1980 and 1987); metallurgy (−78.3 percent over the same period); and chemicals (−48.4 percent between 1980 and 1986). Investments made by public companies in infrastructure were also severely curtailed: Energy (−16.3 percent between 1980 and 1987);

transportation (−50.5 percent between 1980 and 1986); and communications (−8.2 percent between 1980 and 1987).[8]

Trends in the gross formation of fixed capital (GFFC) and GDP at constant prices (Figure 6.4) show that until 1984 these cuts in investment proceeded at a faster pace than the decrease in GDP. This was probably the major factor leading to the adoption of adjustment policies. After a flurry of recovery in 1985–1986 investments once again started to coast downhill until the end of the decade. It is also important to note that investments in machinery and equipment as a proportion of the GFFC—which averaged some 40 percent during the 1980s—slipped throughout the 1980s to reach 25 percent in 1987, climbing again in 1988. This decline may be indicative of reduced investments in the production capacity of industry and the production sector in general.

Information on investments in the private sector is not necessarily sound; however, it appears that they shrank abruptly during the recession at the start of the decade as one of the elements in the adjustment strategies of major companies. Between 1984 and 1986 they eased back up to virtually prerecession levels.[9] Although no precise data are available, all indications are that this recovery was fueled by investments earmarked predominantly for the rationalization of the production

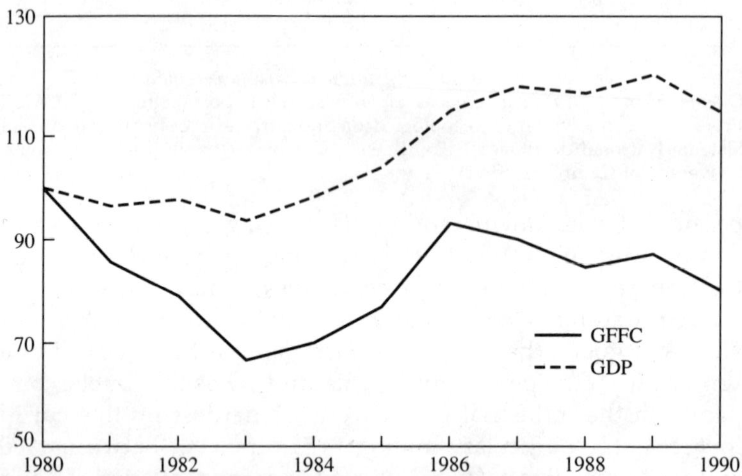

FIGURE 6.4 The Gross Formation of Fixed Capital and GDP at Constant Prices, 1980–1990 (1980 = 100).
SOURCE: IBGE—National Accounts Statistics.

process, through the introduction of technologically more advanced machinery and equipment, industrial automation, and the elimination of bottlenecks in the production process, with only marginal expansion of production capacity. Indirect evidence of this investment characteristic is the fact that of 5,970 numerical-command machine tools in Brazil by 1989, over 90 percent were installed during the 1980s.[10]

Limitations on Efforts at Scientific and Technological Development

The worst consequence of the macroeconomic instability and soaring inflation of the 1980s was that it undermined already limited efforts at scientific and technological development, including education and human resources policy. This effect was directly linked to financial imbalance in the public sector, the main source of funding for science and technology. The 1970s witnessed considerable advances in the development of a science and technology infrastructure, but as the 1980s went on that infrastructure grew politically and financially weaker, culminating in the loss of technical staff and scientists and slashed budgets. The exception to this rule was the group of initiatives implemented between 1986 and 1989 by the now-extinct Ministry of Science and Technology that substantially increased funding for study and research grants and the development of advanced technologies.

Annual outlays on science and technology in Brazil at the end of the 1980s hovered around US$2 billion (Table 6.2), some three-quarters of which were financed by the federal government and the remainder by state-owned companies, public-sector financial agents, state and municipal governments, and the private sector. According to the national science and technology budget data for 1990, the private sector carried some 8 percent of total expenditures.

Table 6.2 also shows that expenditures on industrial technological development absorbed between 45 percent and 50 percent of the total outlays. Because the figure for 1989 (45 percent) is probably the closest to reality, and because industry generates some 35 percent of Brazil's GDP, it is clear that the "technological density" (the ratio of a sector's share of the country's total outlays for science and technology to that same sector's percentage

TABLE 6.2
BRAZIL'S EXPENDITURES ON SCIENCE AND TECHNOLOGY AND ESTIMATES OF THE PERCENTAGE REPRESENTED BY INDUSTRIAL TECHNOLOGICAL DEVELOPMENT
(Amounts in US$ Million/1989)

	Federal government budget (%)			Total[a]		
	(1) Science and technology	(2) Industrial technology	(2)/(1) (%)	(3) Science and technology	(4) Industrial technology	(4)/(3) (%)
1987	1,758	627	35.6	2,380	1,124	47.2
1988	1,712	709	41.4	2,310	1,187	51.4
1989	1,488	493	33.1	2,010	910	45.3

SOURCE: Prepared on the basis of preliminary estimates by the Ministry of Science and Technology (data supplied directly).
[a]To estimate the total expenditures on science and technology, we assumed that they represented the same proportions as those set out in the national science and technology budget for 1990 (initial allocation) and applied them to effective data covering 1987 to 1989 for the federal government budget. These proportions are federal government budget, 74%; state-owned companies, 8%; financial agents, 2%; states and municipalities, 8%; and private sector, 8%. Total expenditures on industrial technology include federal government budget outlays as estimated by the Science and Technology Secretariat of the Presidency of the Republic plus an amount corresponding to 80% of the total outlays of state-owned companies, financial agents, states and municipalities, and the private sector. This percentage (probably overestimated) was obtained by assuming that total science and technology expenditures of state-owned companies and the private sector were earmarked for industrial technology and that 50% of the applications of financial agents and expenditures made by states and municipalities were also set aside for this purpose.

share of GDP)[11] for Brazilian industry is very low (around 1.3) compared to that of the major industrial economies, where this density is some three times greater than the average for the economy. Among the nations in the Group of Seven, for example, industry concentrates some 90 percent of research and development expenditures and generates around one-third of the GDP.[12]

Table 6.3 compares Brazil's level of expenditures on research and development with the levels supported by other countries. It shows that total outlays on science and technology as a proportion of the GDP in Brazil correspond to about one-half that of the Asiatic countries and one-quarter that of the Group of Seven nations. Per capita outlays in Brazil correspond to no more than 4 percent of per capita expenditures on research and development in the major industrial countries (Group of Seven), although they are not too far removed from those of other nations. Private-sector participation in science and technology (or research and development) outlays in Brazil and Latin America has been minor compared to that of other countries, particularly the Asian nations.

There are no available data with which to assess the development of total outlays on science and technology during the 1980s. Table 6.4 summarizes data from the budget of the Brazilian federal government regarding funds administered by

TABLE 6.3
RESEARCH AND DEVELOPMENT OUTLAYS
BY BRAZIL AND OTHER COUNTRIES (MID-1980S)

Outlays on R&D	Brazil[a]	Latin American nations	Mediterranean nations[b]	Asiatic nations[c]	Group of Seven nations[d]
As percent of GDP	0.7	0.6	0.9	1.3	2.7
Per inhabitant (US$)	13.7	12.0	24.0	18.0[e]	346.0
By origin of funds (%)	100.0	100.0	100.0	100.0	100.0
Public sector	92.0	78.8	46.4	35.6	43.1
Private sector	8.0	10.5	49.5	61.4	52.5
Other sources	N/A	10.7	4.1	3.0	4.4
By sector of application of funds (%)	100.0	NA	NA	NA	100.0
Industry	45.0	NA	NA	NA	89.0
Other sectors	55.0	NA	NA	NA	11.0

SOURCE: Brazil—estimates prepared on the basis of preliminary data from the Ministry of Science and Technology, covering total science and technology expenditures. Other countries—ECLAC, *Transformación Productiva con Equidad* (Santiago: United Nations Economic Commission for Latin America and the Caribbean, 1990), 66; and F. Fajnzylber, *Industrialización en America Latina: De la "Caja Negra" al "Casillero Vacio,"* (Santiago: United Nations Economic Commission for Latin America and the Caribbean, 1989), 38–39.

[a]Data for 1989, based on dollar values for that year.
[b]Includes Spain, Greece, Portugal, Turkey and Yugoslavia.
[c]Includes South Korea, Philippines, Hong Kong, Singapore, and Thailand.
[d]Group of Seven consists of U.S.A., Canada, Japan, West Germany, France, Italy, and the U.K.
[e]Excluding Hong Kong.

the Science and Technology Secretariat, formerly the Ministry of Science and Technology. One positive factor, as we have mentioned, is the increase in funding for research and study grants by the National Research Council (CNPq, Conselho Nacional de Pesquisas). However, other science and technology allocations for scientific and technological development were slashed during the late 1980s (see data on the partial total in Table 6.4). For example, the National Fund for the Development of Science and Technology (FNDCT, Fundo Nacional de Desenvolvimento Científico e Tecnológico), which averaged US$180 million annually from 1975 to 1980 and US$250 million from 1981 to 1985, slid down to US$55 million in 1990.[13] Even if we combine the National Fund for the Development of Science and Technology with the Program for the Support of Scientific and Technological Development (PADCT, Programa de Apoio ao Desenvolvimento Científico e Tecnológico, set up in 1984), funding shows a decrease.

TABLE 6.4
BUDGET PERFORMANCE BY PRINCIPAL SOURCES OF SUPPORT FOR SCIENCE AND TECHNOLOGY
(Amounts in US$1,000/1990)

Year	Grants (CNPq)	FNDCT	PADCT	Partial total[a]	Overall total[b]
1980	34.137	177.205	NA	309.072	445.485
1981	37.255	368.411	NA	508.599	652.097
1982	53.510	228.772	NA	362.807	528.128
1983	52.390	191.369	NA	331.931	492.529
1984	48.452	242.089	1.777	369.552	529.361
1985	60.155	219.472	11.191	403.794	591.382
1986	67.411	140.060	34.251	311.395	538.527
1987	125.839	84.053	28.964	390.655	716.925
1988	185.935	96.071	40.916	334.792	727.244
1989	225.470	77.135	36.761	238.192	714.010
1990	223.865	55.204	54.743	213.100	709.397

SOURCE: Prepared on the basis of preliminary estimates by the Science and Technology Secretariat of the Presidency of the Republic (information supplied directly).

[a]Excludes outlays on agency charges and personnel, debt service, and CNPq grants.

[b]Corresponds to the total outlays of the Science and Technology Secretariat of the Presidency of the Republic (personnel and charges, other costs and capital, grants, and debt service).

Structural Problems

In the previous section, we pinpointed the following trends as characteristic Brazilian industrial development since the crisis of the early 1980s:

1. Previous trends were reversed and the pattern of development in force before the crisis lost dynamism, with no new pattern taking shape;
2. Industrial performance was characterized by reduced output for the domestic market, increased export coefficients concentrated in certain industrial segments, and a slower pace of increased productivity;
3. Shrinking investments; and
4. Limitations on efforts to incorporate technical progress.

These trends broadened the technological gap between Brazil and the major industrial economies, increased intersectorial (and in some cases intrasectorial) technological heterogeneity, and accentuated imbalances in the production structure of industry and the economic and social infrastructure. As a result, Brazil may have lost a unique opportunity to jump several stages toward a new technological paradigm—in Freeman's terminology, to "catch up."[14]

The Technological Backwardness of Industry

The technological backwardness of Brazilian industry lies mainly in its outdated equipment and process and product technology, with limited dissemination of innovative management and organizational techniques and reduced investment in research and development. It is also apparent in the insignificant development of industries or activities representing new technological paradigms, with the partial exception of informatics, including automation equipment.

Recent sectorial studies show that, in general and by international standards, Brazilian industry features the following characteristics:[15]

1. It works with technologically outdated equipment and installations. This backwardness is worse in the consumer goods industries (textiles, clothing, footwear, and automobiles), but even more modern industries (basic input

materials and capital goods) show an ever-widening gap in the dissemination of automation equipment;

2. There is a marked and growing lag in process technologies both in continuous process industries, which are behind in the incorporation of automation and computerization of process controls and process design capacity, and in discrete process industries, which lag in the introduction of equipment and automation of manufacture;
3. There is also a marked lag in product technologies. With a few rare exceptions (leading companies that manufacture special steels, auto parts, pulp, automation equipment, informatics, and aircraft), Brazilian industry does not develop product technology, and the list of products is not of a particularly high grade;
4. It provides an extremely low level of expenditures on research and development in relation to sales. Even in industries where research and development outlays are appreciable (informatics, iron and steel, pulp and paper, petrochemicals, auto parts, and aircraft), levels are far lower than the international standard for these industries;
5. It has considerable shortcomings in quality control at both the product and production process levels;
6. It is very backward in the dissemination of management and organizational innovations such as just-in-time, quick response, group technology, and others. These innovations, apart from costing relatively little for the gains in productivity that they engender, represent a first and vital step toward the introduction of modern machinery;
7. Better interaction between the user and the producer is needed, principally in the capital goods industry;
8. Relationships with suppliers are conflictive rather than cooperative; and
9. The standard of relationships between management and workers leaves much to be desired. Labor is still viewed as a cost rather than a basic production resource, meaning that little attention is given to the training and recycling of multipurpose workers.

As a consequence, Brazilian industry has low levels of productivity and high costs, which blunts its competitive edge. It also has other shortcomings, such as slow response to variations in demand, limited production flexibility, and poor product quality and performance. All these factors limit its ability to compete through innovation and the diversification of products.

In keeping with this situation, the pattern by which Brazilian industry is being inserted into the international economy is basically founded on the export of natural resource or energy-intensive commodities and cheap labor-intensive goods. However, even this pattern of integration may well become hard to sustain. International trends in inputs (new materials, new metal alloys, special chemicals, special papers) and consumer goods (higher quality and performance standards, development of new products and models) point to a need to speed up technical progress in these areas.

It is clear that there are exceptions to this pattern. Leading industrial companies that have concentrated on exports are now being forced by the demands of competition on the international market to develop their technological capacity in projects, products, and processes. As a result of this pressure, they have achieved levels of productivity and quality that are competitive on an international scale.

A generalized export model along these lines would, however, be a simplistic, ingenuous strategy. Nor is it simply a matter of developing a model that combines the goals of growth and income distribution. Rather, one must take into account the specific requirements of each sector and industry if one is to avoid reducing the question of technological development to the simplistic objective of "modernizing and automatizing so as to be able to export" and ignoring the "multiple facets of a technologically heterogeneous industrial part, in a socially unbalanced country where low labor costs discourage modernization of installations and production routine in various sectors."[16] Along these lines, "higher real wages challenge companies to seek out production processes that are better organized, more efficient, modern, and automatized." Above all, such a simplistic solution overlooks the need for basic organizational changes in the form of "new work relationships, new schemes of interfirm vertical and horizontal integration, and the effective participation of staff in the mechanisms of business management." These changes "demand a new business mentality, and closely aligned industrial, technological, and educational policy actions."[17]

IMBALANCES IN THE PRODUCTION STRUCTURE

Trends during the 1980s also accentuated two other problems in the production structure: the great heterogeneity of levels of use of installed capacity in specific sectors of the manufacturing industry, and the deterioration of infrastructure services.

The first problem highlights a paradoxical situation. Although current average levels of use are low, because of the crisis in the domestic market, potential bottlenecks exist in certain segments, with extremely high idle capacity in others. The bottlenecks were obviously eased as the recession deepened in 1990–1991, but they continue to be a latent threat in the industrial structure. They are located in industries that produce basic intermediate and primary input materials such as flat rolled steel, petrochemicals, caustic soda (earmarked mainly for the aluminum, pulp, and textile industries), mechanical paste and pulp, paper (including newsprint), and natural, artificial, and synthetic fibers. These segments are important to the structure and dynamics of the processing industry for several reasons. They form the core of high-production chains and export an appreciable part of their output. They are also responsible, directly or indirectly, for a large portion of the foreign exchange revenues from industrial exports, and their investments (with the exception of textile yarns) are large and slow to mature. They depend on public-sector financing or direct investment. The pulp and paper industry is the only one of these segments making new investments in expanding capacity. With a future return to growth, these potential bottlenecks represent sizable hurdles to the industrial production drive, to the development of trade balances, and even to the control of inflation rates, which depends on a recovery of the state's investment and financing capacity and encouragement of private investment, both local and foreign.

On the other hand, the highest levels of idleness are found in segments of the capital goods industry, particularly tractors, bulldozers, and earth-moving machinery; shipbuilding; and railroad equipment. In general, however, the entire capital goods industry, as well as the construction materials industry, is running at levels well below capacity. This situation obviously reflects a reduction in investments, particularly in the public sector (including state-owned companies). The increase in exports in the end of the 1980s was insufficient to offset shrinking domestic demand. High idleness has thus generated additional cost pressures that blunt the competitive edge of these industries and their downstream customers.

The deterioration in infrastructure services (energy, transportation, and communications) has been characterized by bottlenecks, inefficiency, and high costs. In general, these problems have been the result of reduced investments (particularly from the public sector) and outdated rates. The major consequence of this deterioration has been a dramatic plunge in industrial productivity because the availability of efficient infrastructure services at competitive costs is a vital precondition, at the level of the production structure, for competition in industry and the economy as a whole.

A recent National Industry Federation (CNI, Confederção Nacional da Indústria) survey shows that among other factors, the main roadblocks to the expansion of exports are high port and transportation costs. Of the eighteen sectors polled, no less than thirteen pinpointed these costs as the main snags to intensification of their exports, ahead of matters traditionally cited, such as foreign exchange lags, incentives, credit insurance, and excessive red tape.[18]

If these problems are not resolved, efforts to make Brazilian industry competitive will be ineffective. The following paragraphs summarize the situation at the end of 1991.[19]

In the electric power sector, there is no doubt that even a moderate return to growth in the economy will demand a rapid increase in generation and distribution capacity. Current installed capacity is around 50,000 MW, of which 90.7 percent is hydroelectric and the remainder split between steam power and nuclear (at the Angra plant). This means that the country is basically dependent on ongoing investment in hydroelectric plants and transmission lines.

These investments were much reduced between 1983 and 1988. Of the total US$44 billion planned, only US$19 billion was actually invested. This shortfall resulted in scheduling delays for twenty plants, with output planned at 4,000 MW, almost the power of the giant Itaipu hydroelectric plant project. This situation grew worse in 1989, when investments shrank still further to a mere US$1 billion by the third quarter of the year.

The expansion plan for 1990–1999 provided for the construction of seventy-five hydroelectric and steam-powered plants.

Leaving aside (although not without conceding their due importance) environmental issues and land settlement problems arising from the implementation of these plants, the major problem to be faced is financing. The electricity sector's capability to finance itself is limited, on the one hand, by its lack of capital caused by high debt (around US$30 billion) and, on the other, by lagging tariffs throughout the 1980s.

The problem of outdated tariffs actually involves a number of complex issues, including:

1. Rates set uniformly throughout the country, with no consideration for the substantial cost differences among utility companies;
2. Subsidies to the residential consumer of up to 100 kw;
3. Subsidies through special rates for industry in general at the start of the 1980s and in particular for the aluminum processing industry in Brazil's north-northeast region;
4. Late payments to the government utility Eletrobrás from state-owned power distribution companies, topping US$1 billion in the second half of 1989; and
5. Real rate increases during the galloping inflation of the 1980s wiped out by the interval between billing and collection.

An indication of the difficulties ahead for energy supplies is the fact that in 1989 the National Economic and Social Development Bank (BNDES, Banco Nacional do Desenvolvimento Economico e Social) started to turn down financing for projects implementing or expanding production capacity that did not include their own power generation facilities or a guarantee of future energy supplies through a contract signed with utility companies.

As a result of reduced investment in the 1980s the transportation industry is also troubled by a number of serious bottlenecks that threaten the country's economic activity. Maciel outlines the condition of this sector as follows:[20]

1. Twenty percent of the nation's highway network and one-third of its railroad network are in a poor or fair state of conservation, with repairs demanding funding of some US$9 billion;
2. There have been delays in the scheduling of construction work for various airports and for the São Paulo (partial),

Rio de Janeiro, and Belo Horizonte subway systems, and port services have deteriorated;

3. The nation's cargo truck transportation fleet has become obsolete. Medium-size trucks, which carry 51.1 percent of the cargo, have an average age of 11.2 years, and heavy trucks, which carry 20.8 percent, have an average age of 7.9 years. The average age of the total fleet is 9.7 years;
4. The urban bus fleet has become obsolete; and
5. Forty percent of the Federal Railroad Network locomotives are out of service for lack of parts and maintenance.

The most significant problems arising from the condition of the transportation system include the following:

1. There are more accidents, fuel consumption is rising, the operational costs for vehicles are higher, and travel time is longer;
2. Some 14 percent of the volume of grains produced in Brazil is lost every year through lack of suitable transportation, with another 6 percent written off through poor storage conditions, thus forcing food prices up; and
3. In the case of exports and imports, the high cost of domestic transportation is added to freight costs—higher than international standards—and exorbitant port charges.

This situation grows worse still when we consider the need to expand the transportation infrastructure to cope with an eventual return to growth.

Deteriorating communications services affect industrial development more directly because of the diverse and growing interrelationships between the telecommunications industry and various other industrial segments. As in other parts of the infrastructure, the deterioration in telecommunications services is directly linked to cuts in public investments. Having reached 1.08 percent of the GDP in 1977, investments in the federal government's Telebrás system plummeted to 0.4 percent of the GDP in 1980 and shrank still further during the 1980s. The consequences include long delays in getting lines in cities, long-distance calls that give the engaged signal before making the connection, or cutting off during the call, and the repressed demand for seven million telephone lines by the end of the 1980s. According to Telebrás, it will be necessary to invest

US$6.5 billion in two years to return to the level of quality of the early 1980s.

Industrial Policy and Competitiveness: An Assessment

The preceding sections have highlighted problems and raised questions that should guide discussion of an industrial and technological policy for Brazil that will serve as one of the crucial elements in a broader-ranging strategy designed to break the cycle of stagnation. As we have seen, Brazil's industrial dynamism has slackened as the result of an eroding domestic market and despite increasing export coefficients. Levels of investment have been reduced, and efforts to incorporate technical progress are on the wane. All these factors have led to low levels of productivity, technological backwardness, a marked reduction in the growth of the productivity levels of industry itself, and bottlenecks, inefficiencies, and high costs for infrastructure maintenance.

These problems raise some issues that are fundamental to industrial policy. The most important—and the one that will have the most marked effect—is the actual definition of a pattern for development. As Erber recalls:

> The crisis of the 1980s, which stretched out into the current decade, is a crisis of the exhaustion of a pattern of development, this being taken to mean a set of norms that regulate economic and political processes. As a consequence, a return to industrialization, with new norms of production and accumulation also involves modifications in the norms covering incorporation of technical progress, financing, wage ratios, State intervention, and international insertion.[21]

Industrial policy cannot thus be summed up as merely "opening up the economy." If macroeconomically feasible, it may be desirable to lift import restrictions as a component of industrial policy. However, given the current situation of Brazilian industry, protection systems (tariff and nontariff barriers and exchange rate policy) and promotion mechanisms (incentives, subsidies, and financing) should first be rationalized in a carefully timed order of priority selectively articulated and synchronized with the achievement of goals to eliminate technological backwardness and the development of segments representing new technologies. Second, a pattern that combines growth and income distribution seems imperative, not only to help the domestic market return to growth but also to stimulate modernization (because low wages help stretch the working life of obsolete equipment). Third, because a combination of growth and income distribution may condition a pattern of international insertion without necessarily creating it, the country must choose either to specialize in sectors or products in which it has comparative natural advantages (passive insertion) or to seek to create comparative advantages (active insertion). It should be remembered that because of the international trend toward the production and marketing of specialties, the essence of industrial policy must be the development of comparative advantages, even in sectors with natural comparative advantages such as basic input materials. Fourth, depending on the development pattern and the pattern of international insertion, technical progress must be incorporated according to a set of predetermined norms, particularly if the nation needs to develop the capacity to innovate or if it will be limited to acquiring technological capacity for production. The norms adopted then shape the requirements of the country's science and technology infrastructure and its educational system. Finally, it is essential to make the generic conditioning factors of competitiveness (energy, transportation, storage, port services, and telecommunications) as efficient and cost-effective as possible.

In the remainder of this section we will assess the extent to which the guidelines and measures that Brazil's government uses to implement its industrial and foreign trade policy respond to the issues we have discussed and create the conditions necessary for industry to face the challenge of competitiveness.

The first issue involves (1) differences in the timing and relative intensity of the measures used to open the economy and to encourage the modernization of the production structure and technological capacity of Brazilian industry. The opening of the economy began with the import policy reforms instituted at the start of the Collor administration.[22] Administrative restrictions were lifted, surcharges on imports were canceled, exemptions and reductions on the import tax specified in the special import regimes were suspended or eliminated, and reforms in customs tariffs were announced. The purpose of this final item was to have rates for customs duties varying from 0 percent to 40 percent, with average tariffs dropping from 32.2 percent in 1990 to

25.3 percent in 1991, 21.2 percent in 1992, 17.1 percent in 1993, and 14.2 percent in 1994 and have the most common level of tariff reach 20 percent in 1994.[23] In addition, fiscal incentives on income tax for exports were suspended or canceled.[24]

Thus, the liberalization of trade is under way and has made substantial progress toward rationalizing the protection system, making current levels of protection and protected activities transparent, as well as scheduling the reduction of tariff protection, which, although it became the main instrument of protection for industry, proved ineffective as the cruzeiro remained overvalued from March 1990 to the end of 1991.[25] The failure to define a foreign exchange policy that is at least neutral with regard to the protection system generates uncertainty among economic actors regarding the stability of levels of protection and strict compliance with scheduled objectives.

The government has also lightened restrictions in the following ways:

1. In regard to the informatics industry, the end of market reservation is confirmed for October 1992, increased flexibility has been permitted for imports previously allowed into Brazil only with prior agreement, restrictions on the entry of foreign capital have been lifted, and the Software Law has been reformulated and forwarded to Congress;
2. For capital goods, lower mandatory, locally manufactured minimum content levels are required for foreign and domestic firms to qualfiy for fiscal benefits and government loans;
3. The procedures for importing technology have been deregulated;
4. Specific anti-trust and consumer protection laws have been approved; and
5. A new industrial property code that acknowledges patents, brand names, and trademarks for pharmaceutical products, foodstuffs, agroindustrial goods, and biotechnology is before the Congress.

On the other hand, most of the measures designed to encourage domestic industry are behind schedule or poorly defined. Investments in science and technology were intended to rise in 1991 as announced in the Technological Capability Support Program (September 12, 1990) but have instead been reduced because of budget restrictions.[26] Tax incentives earmarked for the technological capability of industry have not yet been approved by Congress; incentives allocated to the modernization of production capacity have already become law, but their implementation depends on congressional approval of the Executive Branch Draft Bill specifying the amount of the tax breaks and the corresponding financing (write-off of expenses); government agency loans for investment, research and development, and exports have also been hamstrung by budget restrictions and conditions imposed on foreign credit by foreign debt negotiations; and finally, the use of the government's procurement policy and the buying power of state-owned companies to bring about technological development, improvements in quality, and so on are also limited by budget restrictions, investment cuts, and other limits on outlays by state-owned companies and the privatization program itself.[27]

It is clear, then, that measures aimed at opening up the economy and those designed to improve the competitive conditions of industry lack synchronization and differ widely in intensity. The main problems lie in two major links between industrial policy and macroeconomic policy: the exchange rate and public finances. The lack of interplay between these policies and the subordination of industrial policy to the current macroeconomic stabilization policy are evident.

The second issue involves the government's support for a pattern of industrial growth, headed by the export sectors, in which "comparative advantages [are] defined on the basis of export positions already consolidated."[28] This industrial policy thus ratifies a pattern of growth and international insertion based on goods that make intensive use of natural resources and energy, as well as low wages—in other words, an industrialized version of the primary export model. The limited dynamism of these sectors in international trade, the low export coefficient of Brazilian industry, and the structural imbalances previously mentioned reduce the possibilities of leveraging growth on the domestic market through these means.

It thus becomes clear that the government has abandoned its initial proposal to "maximize the productivity growth rate" as part of a growth strategy with a hike in real wages.[29] It is clearer still that given the current industrial policy and macroeconomic stabilization plan, a pattern of growth combined with improved income distribution (meaning a greater increase in real wages than in productivity) would be a chimerical objective. Consequently, the following outcomes are possible: (1) the modernization of production capacity may well be undermined, given the inevitable comparisons of its costs with the costs of labor; and (2) the expansion of the domestic market could be postponed. The intensification of political and economic difficulties related to macroeconomic stabilization accentuates these trends.

Third, although the option that the government has chosen amounts to a passive international insertion, the Industrial Competitiveness Program emphasizes the technological enhancement of export sectors (modernization, product upgrading, and improved quality), along with the development of the "sectors that generate and disseminate technical progress," but does not target specific industries. As a result, its actions are limited to general recommendations that will provide a basis for discussions on sectorial strategies by the Business Competitiveness Commission.[30] These recommendations emphasize (1) technological and organizational modernization and increased internationalization of sectors with comparative advantages; and (2) the establishment of joint-ventures between Brazilian and foreign companies.

It is clear that export sectors' technological upgrading, tied to the development of sectors that generate technical progress, presupposes the development of technological capability by Brazilian firms in these areas. For this purpose, the search for knowledge must go beyond the simple capacity to produce; it must include the ability to innovate. This ability demands an adequate science and technology infrastructure and an educational system with a strong research and postgraduate basis, as well as protection for innovative Brazilian companies. However, these requirements have not been met in Brazil today. Funding for the nation's science and technology infrastructure has been slashed, producing a net outflow of technicians and scientists,[31] as well as a drop in political support. The educational system is in a state of penury, and protection for Brazilian companies has been made politically infeasible by the lifting of restrictions on the entry of foreign capital and importation of technology.

Fourth, and finally, very little has been done to improve the general conditions of competitiveness by straightening out the bottlenecks, inefficiencies, and high costs of infrastructure services (energy, transportation, warehousing, port services, and telecommunications). The Collor government did no more than forward to Congress a draft bill designed to deregulate port services and introduce a tax on oil imports to finance repair of the country's highway network. Given the present budgetary restrictions and the difficulties involved in implementing a privatization program in these areas, these problems are likely to remain as serious hurdles to the improved competitiveness of Brazilian industry and the growth of the nation's economy as a whole.

Final Remarks

Brazilian industry today faces a lack of dynamism, technological backwardness, marked imbalances in its production structure, and an inefficient infrastructure. To open up the nation's economy without at least attempting to solve these problems at the same time and with the same intensity of effort is to create uncertainty and to accentuate the trend toward recession. In fact, the lifting of restrictions was badly planned and hampered by political issues (negotiation of the nation's foreign debt, and the political affirmation of its new government) and economic policy (macroeconomic stabilization). However, the most serious problem is the lack of a corresponding effort to encourage technological capability. This deficiency will inevitably delay both the entrance of Brazilian industry into the new technological paradigms and the definition of a new pattern of industrial development.

Notes

1 The author thanks Werner Baer and Riordan Roett, two participants in the conference for which this chapter was written, for their useful comments. Werner Baer's editorial suggestions were also helpful.

2 See João Furtado, "Produtividade na Industria Brasileira: Padrões Setoriais e Evolucáo—1975/80," (Master's diss., Institute of Economics, State University of Campinas, 1990).

3 F. Sarti and J. Furtado, *Estrutura e Exportacões Industriais nos Anos Oitenta: Elementos para uma Caracterização*, Research Report of the IPT/FECAMP Project "Desenvolvimento Tecnológico da Indústria e a Constituição de um Sistema Nacional de Inovação no Brasil" (Campinas, Brazil: Institute of Economics, State University of Campinas, 1991), 6.

[4] See Sarti and Furtado, *Estrutura e Exportacões Industriais,* 13; based on data on the Brazilian manufacturing industry from the Instituto Brasileiro de Geografia e Estadística (IBGE).

[5] W. Suzigan, "Condicionantes e Princípios Básicos de uma Estratégia Industrial Brasileira para a Década de Noventa," *Anais do Simposio EPUSP sobre Modernização Tecnológica e Política Industrial* (São Paulo: Escola Politecnica/USP, 1989), 379–404.

[6] See R. Baumann, "Ajuste Externo—Experiencia Recente e Perspectivas para a Próxima Década," *Para a Década de 90—Prioridades e Perspectivas de Políticas Púbicas* (Brasilia: IPEA/IPLAN 1989), 1–27. According to Baumann, total incentives and subsidies as a proportion of the FOB value of exports of manufactured goods dropped to 45 percent in 1980 after the IPI/ICM tax credit premium was canceled. In 1981–1982 this proportion rose to 75 percent with return of the credit premium and increased financial subsidies, leveling out at 54 percent after 1983.

[7] C. S. Maciel, *Padrão de Investimento Industrial nos Anos Noventa e suas Implicacões para a Política Tecnológica,* Research Report of the IPT/FECAMP Project "Desenvolvimento Tecnológico da Indústria e a Constituição de um Sistema Nacional de Inovação no Brasil" (Campinas, Brazil: Institute of Economics, University of Campinas, 1990), 78.

[8] Data from Maciel, *Padrão de Investimento Industrial,* 79–81.

[9] Cf. data in Maciel, *Padrão de Investimento Industrial,* 80. However, it should be noted that data on investment in the private sector were obtained from figures for GFFC and public-sector investments only for 1980–1986.

[10] Mariano F. Laplane, *Diagnóstico da Indústria Brasileira de Máquinas-Ferramenta,* Research Report of the IPT/FECAMP Project, "Desenvolvimento Tecnológico da Indústria e a Constituição de um Sistema Nacional de Invocação no Brasil" (Campinas, Brazil: Institute of Economics, University of Campinas, 1990).

[11] The concept of technological density was suggested by F. Fajnzylber in *Industrialización en América Latina: De la "Caja Negra" al "Casillero Vacio,"* United Nations, Economic Commission for Latin America and the Caribbean, ECLAC Report no. 60 (Santiago, 1989), chap. 2.

[12] Cf. data from Fajnzylber, *Industrialización en América Latina,* 38–39.

[13] All amounts correspond to expenditures made, estimated by the Science and Technology Secretariat of the Presidency of the Republic in US$ for 1990.

[14] C. Freeman, "New Technology and Catching Up," *The European Journal of Development Research* 1 (June 1989): 85–99.

[15] Such studies were carried out at the University of Campinas (UNICAMP) for the project entitled Technological Development of Industry and the Constitution of the National System of Innovation in Brazil. This project was sponsored by the São Paulo state government and coordinated by Luciano G. Coutinho and Wilson Suzigan (Campinas, Brazil: Institute of Economics, University of Campinas, 1991). Sectoral studies covered the most important segments in the areas of basic input materials and intermediate goods (steel, aluminum, pulp and paper, and petrochemicals), capital goods, the electronic complex (informatics, semiconductor components, automation equipment), the automobile industry (including auto parts), and nondurable goods (textiles, clothing, and footwear). The research reports are available at IE/UNICAMP, Caixa Postal 6135,

CEP 13081—Campinas, S. P., Brazil. A book summarizing the results of the overall research project will be published in the near future.

16 Maciel, *Padrão de Investimento Industrial,* 108.

17 Maciel, *Padrão de Investimento Industrial,* 108–109.

18 CNI—Confederação Nacional da Indústria, *Abertura Comercial e Estratégia Tecnológica: A Visão de Líderes Industrialis Brasileiros* (Rio de Janeiro: CNI, 1991), 13–16.

19 This summary is based on the study by C. S. Maciel, *Investimento e Modernização Tecnológica na Indústria Brasileira durante a Decada de Oitenta,* Research Report of the SCTDE/SP-FECAMP Project "Competitividade da Indústria e a Constituição de um Sistema Nacional de Inovação no Brasil" (Campinas, Brazil: Institute of Economics, University of Campinas, 1990), 14–23.

20 Maciel, *Investimento e Modernização,* 20–21.

21 F. S. Erber, "A Política Industrial—Paradigmas Teóricos e Modernidade," in M. C. Tavares, A. Teixeira, and M. V. J. Penna, eds., *Aquarella do Brasil* (Rio de Janeiro: Rio Fundo Editors, 1990), 107.

22 Provisional Measure no. 158 (March 15, 1990), regulated by Law no. 8,032 and edict no. 56 issued by the Ministry of Economy, Treasury, and Planning.

23 Cf. Ministry of the Economy, Treasury, and Planning, National Economy Secretariat, Department of Foreign Trade/Tariff Technical Coordination Section, "A Política Tarifária no Período 1991–94," n.d.

24 Provisional Measure no. 161 (March 15, 1990), regulated by Law no. 8,034. The regional development incentives were reinstated through Decree Law no. 10, dated April 17, 1991.

25 See CNI—Confederação Nacional da Indústria, Departamento Econômico, *Informe Conjuntural* 75 (May 1992), 32. According to the estimate by CNI, the lag in the foreign exchange rate (measured against a basket of currencies without taking external inflation into account) reached 44 percent in April 1990 and 21.6 percent in August 1991. On September 30, 1991, the Central Bank of Brazil intervened to devalue the cruzeiro by 16.1 percent, reducing the lag to 7.6 percent. In April 1992, however, it had risen again to 13 percent.

26 F. S. Erber, "A Política Indústrial e de Comercial Exterior: Uma Avaliação," in *Perspectivas da Economia Brasileira—1992* (Rio de Janeiro: IPEA, 1991), 305–33.

27 Erber, "A Política Indústrial e de Comercial Exterior," 305–33.

28 Industrial Competitiveness Edict no. 123, issued by the Ministry of the Economy, Treasury, and Planning on February 27, 1991.

29 See the Exposition of Motives accompanying Provisional Measure no. 158, dated March 16, 1990. According to FEISP (São Paulo State Federation of Industries) data, the average real wage in June 1991 was 20.3 percent below the average for 1988. See CNI—Confederação Nacional da Indústria, Departamento Econômico, "Preços Relativos, Indexação e Políticas de Estabilização: Notas sobre a Experiencia Recente," August 1991, 10.

30 Established on February 27, 1991, together with the initiation of the Industrial Competitiveness Program.

31 See, for example, "Crises Provoca Evasão de Técnicos no Centro de Pesquisa da TELEBRAS," *Folha de São Paulo,* February 26, 1991.

Epilogue:

Unfinished Reforms

José Augusto Guilhon Albuquerque

Since the end of military rule in 1985 Brazil has failed to address the need for economic reform and political stability. José Sarney[1] started no fewer than three programs of economic stabilization during his five years as president.

As each economic reform program was prepared, Brazil was on the verge of hyperinflation and stagnation as a result of the failure of the previous stabilization program. On each occasion, too, the reform included a package of "heterodox" macroeconomic measures ranging from wage and price freezes to devaluation and adoption of a new currency.

Fernando Collor de Mello, the first president to be elected by direct popular vote since the election of Jânio Quadros in 1960, was particularly concerned with two of his campaign pledges: killing the "inflation tiger" with one single shot, as he used to phrase it, and modernizing the country to join the club of first world nations, which meant trade liberalization, deregulation, and privatization. Together the two pledges amounted to an urgent need for economic reform.

When Fernando Collor de Mello resigned, after transferring the acting presidency to then–vice-president Itamar Franco, as a result of an impeachment trial by the Senate, he found himself in a position very similar to the one he was in the day he began his quest for Brazil's presidency. Then, as now, he lacked the minimum requirements to lead a complex, modern democratic society such as Brazil: he had no party support, no credibility with the elites, no experienced executive team to rely on, no workable agenda for gathering a stable coalition, no links with organized labor or grassroots social movements, no respect from the military, and none of the personal maturity needed to govern.

During his brief tenure Collor lost the ability to secure the favorable media coverage that had dramatically enhanced his popularity during the campaign—his major and sole asset. Like the Bourbons during their time in exile, Collor learned nothing and forgot nothing from his experience in power.

One must learn from Collor's errors, which were many and huge, but the true challenge is to understand how this man could have been elected, despite his mistakes and his lack of fitness for the presidential office, and why the Brazilian political system favored his kind of leadership, so conspicuously prone to populism and confrontation.

Brief as it was, Collor's administration started and restarted on three different occasions, marked each time by the appointment of a new cabinet. Each of the three assumed office amid a deep political crisis. A brief review of those crises will help us determine how Collor failed in government: he relied on the very qualities that had proved important to his electoral victory. Ultimately, in any comment on the administration, one must conclude with a plea to change a system that selects electoral winners who are predictable losers when challenged by the need to govern.

In his first effort Collor was unable to appoint a cabinet that would meet both his pledge to lead with the best and the brightest and to govern with a sound congressional majority. The campaign tone he maintained before the inauguration, bashing "professional politicians" and pledging not to appoint cabinet or other top officials who had served in previous governments, estranged him from experienced moderate leaders and made it difficult for their political parties officially to enter the government.

Moreover, his small team of campaign issue advisors proved unable to maintain strong control over economic policies because they lacked minimal political ability and executive experience. They were not accountable to any public constituency, but they were the only people he knew and trusted. Knowing this, several well-known personalities invited to head the new, all-powerful Ministry of Economy declined to serve.

As succeeding crises demonstrated, Collor's surprising ability to gather a winning electoral coalition was not adaptable to creating and implementing a governing strategy. The best example was his handling of economic reform. First, Collor appointed his chief campaign adviser to head the new, strategic Ministry of Economy. A young, inexperienced teacher of economic history, with scarcely any executive experience either in public or private administration, Zelia Cardoso set up an economic team that was the very image of herself. Second, despite—or rather because of—its overwhelmingly ambitious goals, the reform program was suffused with inconsistencies and complications. Its expected success was based on Collor's presumed ability to sell it to the public, which proved much more difficult than he anticipated. Third, the most fashionable features of the program, namely the freezing of prices, wages, and financial assets, were given top priority, while the structural reforms, such as deregulation, privatization, and trade liberalization, were relegated to a minor role. Months later, responding to a growing criticism of its inability to foster long-range economic reforms, Collor's economic team sent to Congress the *pacotão* (monster package), aimed at creating the legal basis for the reforms. In fact, it amounted to only a vague framework, including both specific measures and statements of intentions, with no fixed deadlines or defined voting procedures.

Collor's second attempt was precipitated by the need to replace several cabinet members charged with corruption and appointed either for their emblematic significance or in return for their campaign support. These included the ministers of labor (a former union leader), health (campaign supporter in an important region), and social welfare (a long-time aide to Collor's family). Moreover, the ministers of justice (the former chairman of the new Constitution's reporting committee at the National Constituent Assembly) and the economy (a former campaign adviser) were engaged in a conspicuous and reprehensible love affair. The minister of education (former chairman of the Senate investigatory committee on government corruption), besides facing minor charges of corruption, was believed by the government to be insufficiently responsive to pork-barreling demands.

Again, Collor was unable to set up either a stable coalition to support the government in Congress or an issue-oriented executive team. Instead, he turned again to a mix of symbolic appointments (a renowned cardiologist to lead the Ministry of Health, a successful scholar and university administrator as head of the Ministry of Education, and an internationally respected diplomat to deal with the issue of external debt) and ad hoc coalitions with specific groups of limited influence in Congress.

Agreement between Collor and the major moderate political parties proved impossible. The cabinet appointees did not represent their parties; they were supposed to respond to the president's personal leadership. Any attempt to develop a party coalition in support of the administration failed because administration officials believed that the combination of popular support and the president's capacity to bargain for individual support in Congress on a day-to-day basis apparently precluded the need for Collor to compromise with the opposition. He would go it alone.

Collor's third attempt stemmed from earlier charges of corruption that eventually produced the scandal that cost him the presidency. His brother, Pedro Collor de Mello, had not yet unveiled the personal involvement of the president in a network of influence peddling set up by his campaign treasurer, Paulo César Farias. But three ex–Cabinet members were already under investigation, and a series of charges had been made by different sources against presidential aides of various executive levels.

Even though the president had just named a new minister, the secretary of government, who was responsible for political coordination of the executive branch, he forced the collective resignation of his cabinet. The resignation occurred amid a general feeling of moral and political crisis. In a very unusual move for a presidentialist regime, the leadership of the major parties subsequently met to discuss means to ensure the country's governability.

Aware of his new political coordinator's inability to make rapid appointments to a new cabinet, Collor took the opportunity to announce an entirely new government, which was supposed to emerge from the broad political consultations. Again, the talks with the leadership of the parties were unsuccessful, and this exposed the government's inability to secure vital political support.

Some veteran politicians did join the government without the official commitment of their parties. Hence the representatives of their parties in Congress had the advantages of officialdom but no obligation to support the government. Again, some symbolic appointments provided prestige but not political or popular support and, above all, no guarantee of efficient governance. As before, some strategic positions were reserved for faithful friends and followers.

Having been elected without the confidence of the political establishment, facing overt hostility from the most active union leadership, absent political party or congressional support, Collor relied exclusively on his media image to reverse the odds against him. His astonishing electoral victory had led him to disregard the importance of the political system, to despise and hence to underestimate the power of the political elites, and to ignore the public's ability to resist image manipulation.

Under the best of circumstances, the combined impact of executive power and proportional representation in the lower house (Chamber of Deputies) weakens party loyalty in Brazil and makes it necessary for the president to develop personal congressional support. He can do so by building party coalitions or by getting members of Congress to cross party lines. Collor rapidly developed an ad hoc congressional coalition to support his government. Although too weak to give him a solid and stable majority, the coalition was strong enough to block the initiatives of a divided opposition and to build an occasional day-to-day majority. Dazzled by his own success, Collor did nothing to build on his ad hoc support to create a governing majority. Consequently, he had to rebuild his support every step of the way—a process of increasing political cost.

Machiavelli makes an important distinction, often misunderstood, between the assumption of political power and its conservation. While the former may be achieved either by *fortuna* or *virtu*, or by a combination of both, the latter requires *virtu*'s ability to mold events to suit one's goals, which in turn requires the ability to subordinate immediate personal goals to a greater, long-term objective, namely the consolidation and stabilization of power.

A similar distinction can be made between the ability to build a coalition of votes to win elections and the ability to build a governing coalition to lead a democratic political body. The former may be achieved either by popular or institutional support, or by a combination of both—when popular support is the ultimate goal—but the latter may be achieved only through the creation of an institutionalized governing system.

In a modern presidential campaign one needs a very broad program to build a coalition, while governing requires a consistent one; in a campaign one needs to address conflicting agendas, while in governing one needs to choose between alternatives; in a campaign one needs to translate political support into popularity, while in governing one needs to do the opposite; in a campaign one needs to accommodate different interests whose only common goal is to elect the candidate, while in governing one must accommodate diverging goals. A strategy that meets the first set of requirements does not necessarily meet the second. When a political system selects its highest leadership only on the basis of electoral appeal—ignoring the leader's qualifications, or lack thereof, as a governor—something is basically wrong with its political institutions.

From the beginning Collor chose to act in office as he did during the campaign. He kept the same goals and used the same methods. He used the media—mainly the electronic media—as his major and sole instrument of government, turning his back on Congress, the political parties, the business community, the labor unions, the judiciary, the military. . . .

Two and a half years before his resignation, I wrote an appraisal of Collor's first six months in government. It was my conclusion that he lacked the essentials: solid party support, the confidence of the establishment, and the neutralization of his opponents, and I stand by that assessment. In contrast to today, however, Collor at least did not lack what proved to be superfluous: popularity.[2]

Notes

1 Vice-president–elect José Sarney was sworn in as acting president in lieu of the ailing president-elect Tancredo Neves, who died before being inaugurated as the first civilian to succeed the long series of military rulers since 1964.

2 J. A. Guilhon Albuquerque, "The Essential Is Lacking," *Folha de São Paulo*, March 15, 1990, A3: "Falta-lhe, portanto, o essencial, isto é, apoio partidário sólido, confianca das elites, neutralização dos adversários. Porque o supérfluo, isto é, a popularidade, ainda não lhe tem faltado."

Index

Page numbers in italics refer to tables.